GW00499979

Dawning

A Journey of Life Change, Regrets & Hard Lessons Learned

Barry Heaton

Kindle Direct Publishing

First published in Great Britain in 2021

Copyright © 2021 Barry Heaton

Paperback ISBN 9798515589981

Dawning

A Journey of a Life
Change, Regrets & Hard Lessons Learned

'Were you a baby – boomer born into a Christian family and struggled during your early years to find your own faith and your own walk with God?

Have you been through countless churches - still find church a huge challenge yet know deep down you love the church?

Have you been on many mountain tops and through many valleys with God – experiencing wonderful highs and terrible lows – including devastating personal loss?

After all this do you still love Jesus with a passion and are you still determined to run the race – whatever the cost?

Then this book is for you – read Barry's story and be wonderfully encouraged!!!'

Eric Cairns – friend and fellow church planter and pastor.

'If you need inspiration & encouragement for your onward journey, then read how Barry experienced the overwhelming love & sufficiency of God in every step he took and every problem he faced.'

Gordon & Jackie Wright, Founders of Plymouth CrossLine

Acknowledgments

Heartfelt thanks to good friends Betty Tully and Emily
Julian for their patience
and editing skills,
and also Beth Jordan for her skills producing the cover.

Cover photograph, Sunrising over Pednvounder cliffs,
the far west of Cornwall.

Disappointments have become opportunities for learning
many practical lessons so relevant to followers of Jesus, but
also for those who are not yet sure of the relevance of a
living, dynamic Jesus, but are willing for their own
'Dawning.'
This is not a story of despair, far from it: it's about victory,
hope and a wonderful future.

Emily Julian - school teacher and mother.

Table of Contents

Preface

I lie on the floor, totally overwhelmed and amazed. I see myself as a tiny strand, yet woven into a vast bale of fabric, part of which I see spread out before me. This closely woven, richly multi-coloured cloth is of surpassing beauty exquisite to the touch. Awesome to behold. I don't see me any more - I'm a part of something truly wonderful. Nothing is wasted. Every strand is of immense, unique value in this spectacular work of a truly loving Holy God!

What a privilege it has been. I look back over my life. As I reflect what God has been doing. I weep, I'm stirred deeply as I consider the times of change He has allowed me to witness and to experience. In writing these words, how can I not stop and worship Him for all He is and has done in me.

I've been living through a profound time of on-going renewal, even restoration in something so close to God's heart: His Body, His Church, that His Son Jesus died for! There have been exceptional peaks and, yes, so many troughs. But there is so much more to come. He's not finished yet. He is still doing it now! But I must resist the temptation of looking for just 'the next big new thing' that He is going to do, like a revival of the past.

Dare I really believe it? That, despite so much good in these past sixty years or so, He has not finished yet? I've this strong feeling, that, just as our culture and the world's culture has been working through seismic shaking during

this period, along with exponential change that is only speeding up, so our awesome
God is not lagging behind in caring for and building His Church. Even now He's building on that reformation that started back when I was a kid!

However, over these years there are so many people, good people, committed people, people of real value, gifting, integrity and faith now carrying so much pain and great disappointment in church, that had started so well - and yet now they are no where to be seen. Disappeared off the stage. Many wonderful brothers and sisters in Christ now no longer walking with Jesus, even years later.

Despite all, as I reflect, why did I not turn my back on it all? Instead I am filled with an overwhelming, logically unreasonable excitement. Our Father is building on our brokenness and even disillusion! In His hands the bumps in the road are a springboard for the change He is bringing, for so much more in the days and years ahead. 'Where sin increased, grace abounded all the more.' (Rom 5:20)

It has been such a gradual realisation of the significance of the four 'Big Cs.' Such a slow dawning, only made possible by painful experiences; bit by bit, exposing my many pre-conceived ideas. How easy it has been, to fit in with what is culturally accepted without question, being driven by my damaged identity that has demanded my performance. However not all of the 'Big Cs' are negative; final realisation of the profound significance of them, has been truly wonderful for me, however, we'll come to these later.

I know only too well what it is like to struggle with trusting my Heavenly Father. So many times I've been confident that 'I've got it licked' only for doubt to knock

hard on the door and then to knock it down! Is it possible that at some time in the future I will have finally got doubt beaten? This has been just one
of the issues I've had to face, through my life-journey. I'm very aware of times I've failed in this and so many other areas. But so much has been learnt along the way. What an amazing journey it's been so far. This life has turned out to be truly dynamic. Join me as I re-visit my journey again. It's never been boring!

For the longest time I could not face my mistakes, especially the dreadful mistakes. To face up to my failings and the damage I've caused was too much of a threat to my identity. It is so good that I've come to realise that the more I have faced up to my shortfalls, the more I have discovered about the amazing God
who is seen in the face of Jesus. So many of my discoveries have been like the slow dawning of a brand new day, as the sun rises in the east. What patience God has had with me! I think back to that chorus I learnt while a pre-teenager, based on the parable of Jesus.

The wise man built his house upon the rock
The wise man built his house upon the rock
The wise man built his house upon the rock
And the rain came tumbling down

The rain came down and the floods came up
The rain came down and the floods came up
The rain came down and the floods came up
And the house on the rock stood firm.

At a very early age God started to build a very good foundation in my life, Jesus.

However the building of this house has taken a lifetime to build; even now it's not quite finished.

Chapter 1

Early Days

First Memories

I must have been two or three years old. The sense of
excitement toddling along this cinder pathway going straight
in front of me, fields on the left and bushes to the right.
Bright eyed and bushy tailed I'm off to explore. Vividly I
remember the sudden sense of panic, stopping, looking back
- I was all on my own. Everything was unfamiliar. I'm lost!
For some reason I didn't go any further forward and was
going back the way I'd come, until I saw my mother ahead,
at the beginning of the cinder track, shouting at me through
torrents of tears of desperation.

As a family we were viewing a bungalow in Surrey.
Behind the row of houses were woods and the playing fields
of the Goblin factory. While my parents and older brother
had been seeing the rooms with the estate agent, I'd
explored the wonderful back garden and found a gate at the
top, and managed to open it enough to squeeze through. If
I'd panicked, parents had panicked big time. In an area they
didn't know, with woods off to the left and acres of fields to
the right, with a track going goodness knows where!
When my distraught mother scooped me up, I felt a warm
security, but also a high-pitched, tear-filled something was
coming from my mother. Then my father was there.

I've often wondered why certain things, even at such a very early age can make a deep impression and often affect us, in years to come. About a year after we had moved to that bungalow there was another memory of even greater significance for me.

It was a Saturday afternoon, my Dad had got back from work and it was just before teatime. I remember bouncing up and down on my bed, singing at the top of my voice a CSSM chorus, while waving my hands to the actions, with my father sat next to me, on the bed, joining in.

Wide wide as the ocean, high as the heavens above
deep deep as the deepest sea is my Saviours' love,
I though so unworthy still am a child of His care,
for His word teaches me that His love reaches me everywhere.

I am in no doubt at all, that from that time on, I was aware of Jesus in my life. This amazing God had responded to the simple desire within a young child like me. Looking back, something very real had started for little Barry! In the years that followed, growing up in a Christian context with the enthusiastic call to make a decision and to give your life over to Jesus and be 'born again'; the necessary step for becoming a Christian became a real puzzle and problem for me. It took me many years, to finally realise, the impossibility of getting into a room you're already in! The reality was, however, that my awareness of Jesus and His presence only grew from those early years, even though my starting experience seemed not to fit with the way it was for most people who became Christians - I didn't have a proper 'testimony'!

Formative Years

I struggled through much of my pre-teen years and even into my teens. I felt odd.

The Crusaders bible class movement of those years had a profound effect on me - mainly for good! My mum and dad, independently of each other, had become Christians through the movement in their teens. As a consequence after the war my father re-connected and became an enthusiastic leader in the local bible class.

As a rising seven year old I joined the Juniors in Crusaders, meeting every Sunday afternoon in Leatherhead for an hour long meeting. The first half comprised a hymn or two then singing of choruses, a Bible reading, a Bible quiz, maybe a testimony of how someone came to believe and become a Christian - and of course the inevitable 'notices' of what exciting activities were coming up locally or nationally. In the second half of the meeting we were split into three age groups, juniors, inters and seniors.

I am so sorry Michael Pinkess. In the juniors I made your life a misery. I was definitely the ring-leader of the group. Bit by bit we would pull our chairs up to the front, around Mr Pinkess, as he tried to teach us about the bible story of the week. We'd slide the chairs closer and closer until he could not move, all the while looking straight at him and tittering at his discomfort.

Years later, when a student, I spent a Sunday taking the services at the Baptist church in which he and his family were members. Bless him! They graciously hosted me for the day between morning and evening services. I had the opportunity of apologising for my dreadful behaviour back in those days and thanking him for his incredible patience with such a reprobate. But back to this seven year old. At

16

home, every Sunday after the meeting came the inevitable. My dear father, with growing tones of severity, reprimanding me for my inappropriate behaviour and leading the others astray, again. Worse still I was the leader's son! I deserved it of course, but something was starting that only grew inside me over the years to come. I was 'disapproved of, beyond the pail.' I was a child, but maybe with an inordinate sense of fun and definitely an appetite for adventure, who loved leading others into it too.

Within a few years the inevitable was happening. School term had finished, it was the holidays, yippee. But three times a year there was the unavoidable brown envelope landing on the doormat. I'd see it and dread the homecoming of father, from work that evening: then the call to the lounge. I'd sit in one of the armchairs. He always stood. Disapproval oozed out of every pore, along with the scowl of despair and the school report in his hand, reading the inevitable conclusion of the report: 'could do better' then, father's response, 'Oh Barry!'

He was right of course and I've never doubted my dad wanted the best for me, but he never knew of the affect that was building inside me. As the years passed I knew that I was a failure - fit for nothing.

My dad worked in a chemical company in the East End of London for the years after the Second World War. The ninety minute commute each way, for a five and a half day working week, coping with two children, a wife and long evenings given over to study, resulted in the almost inevitable nervous breakdown. However persistence paid off and he finally qualified as a Chartered Company Secretary.

A year or so later the company was bought out by Pfizers, an American pharmaceutical company breaking into

17

the UK, with a massive new plant on the south Kent coast. The chemical company dad had been with ceased to exist; everyone lost their jobs except two, my father and one other. The new pharmaceutical company needed a Company Secretary for the new Board of Directors. Dad was given the choice, re-locate to Kent, or get paid off. It was a no-brainer.

A New Decade of Profound Change

It was the last year before my teen years, December 31st 1959; mother, father, brother, sister and I arrived early that evening to spend the night at the very smart Royal Albion Hotel, on the Broadstairs seafront. It was the day we'd moved from our Surrey home, ready for completion the next day, January the first 1960. The morning came, keys were collected for the new house on Stanley Road, along with it a whole new world: a new year, a new decade a new beginning with the new opportunities that I really did need.

What a decade it turned out to be: new schools, pirate radio stations, adolescence, flower power, mods and rockers, pot, 'free love' (as if love is ever free - it's always costly), trousers with crazy flares, rock music and massive free open air concerts in Hyde Park and eventually Radio One. In fact seismic cultural change!

My brother couldn't change schools as his A Levels were just starting but he could move to the Boarding House. I was the problem. Two months before the move I'd been off school for weeks due to concussion on the rugby field. Add to this my school record was rubbish - what to do with me? I was now 12 years old. The school had suggested I sit the 13 Plus exam. I failed disastrously! What to do? It was totally unthinkable for the family culture to even consider the local secondary modern. As a last resort a prep school was located. From Broadstairs it was a daily train ride with just five terms to get up to speed, in order to sit the Common Entrance Exam for entrance to a halfway reasonable public school in a nearby town.

They would have me, but it was not going to be an easy journey, and so I found out: learn Latin from scratch, profound improvement in French, maths, English, in fact everything, in order to pass the entrance exams. Homework was done at the school and term time meant the train ride home six days a week getting back at 7.30 pm. Worse still, holidays meant being tutored by father five days a week. If I hadn't got it before, I learnt it then - I was not an academic! As I tried to face the expectations, this period of time was just another demonstration of the failure I was.

I did become proficient at one thing: testing my father's patience and learning to cope with his continued disappointment with me. Good did result however - Dad certainly improved his Latin no end and I definitely honed his patience. In the last term the results came back. Amazingly I had passed. Even more amazing, when the new school started I wasn't even in the bottom grade for my year!

My heavenly Father had opened up a whole new world for me, a fresh start with what turned out to be so many wonderful life-changing opportunities. Yet, much later, was to come the affect my loving, caring, earthly father's disapproval had on my inner identity. But come it would: the scales were filling .

Chapter 2

No Walk in Park

What a journey it is seeking to follow Jesus! Truly I've experienced so many highs and lows. So much excitement. God has been so good time and again and I know it. And yet, also so much disappointment; so many mistakes; so many heartbreaks. Surely plenty of good reasons for disillusionment. Seeking to follow this Jesus has not been easy, dare I say much of the time, and many of the obstacles have certainly been in me!

Yet in all of this are times of praise, worship and wonder at our amazing God breaking through, making the difference, but then feeling let down by people. Yet there are also times of being so aware how much I've let people down and definitely let Him down. Times of reflecting and feeling so disappointed with myself. Regret, shame, a failure, useless! Saddest of all believing I must try harder!

If in any way you can relate to any of this - hold on, I want to encourage you! I'm deeply puzzled. Why haven't I given up? How come that in it all, my vision and passion for His church has only grown and developed? Sadly, so many wonderful people have given up on this Jesus and completely walked away from church! And for me so many justifications to do the same.

Walking with my extra special partner and wife through nine agonising years, witnessing her gradual

20

disappearance before my very eyes, bit by bit taken by a relatively rare terminal illness.

Coping with the additional grief of 'staying strong' for the two daughters still at home fighting through their teenage years while losing their mother. Then all the pressures, conflicts and tensions of leading in church life.

What sort of cruel taskmaster is this God? Surely, walk away from this Church and the people who seemed to be a million miles from everything that Jesus said and did? Everything that turned the Apostle Paul up-side-down?

But I didn't! It defies human logic! The opposite happened.

Half way through my adult life with so much experience under my belt, with still so much passion for the gospel and to see his church flourish and grow, He took me 'in hand!' Rather He 'took me by the hand.'

He began to give me that new soft heart that I had been crying out for over the past decade. He began to give me radically new glasses, rather eyes! Eyes to see him differently. Eyes to see myself is such a different way. Eyes to see his heart for church in a different way. Eyes to see people in a different light. To see and feel his heart for the hurting world. He began to answer my long standing prayer: 'Father, break my heart with what breaks yours.' But I must not jump ahead - there's still more to come before we get there.

Bit by bit over a period of years a whole new perspective was informing and shaping me. I was starting to face my many mistakes, the failures and the weaknesses in me and in my past. It was the beginning, and just the beginning, of whole new understanding and experience of my amazing heavenly Father and his ability to transform!

Even me! Don't get the wrong end of the stick though. That wasn't the end of the mistakes and disappointments!

Best stop here! A 'Let the Reader Beware' warning. If you want to read a 'victory all the way,' quick fix-it, wizzi-wiz testimony that won't challenge pre-conceived ideas and won't imply and demand change, then please put this down now! I won't be offended.

But if you do read on my hope is that through my journey our amazing heavenly Father may just speak to you and encourage you in your adventure with Him.

So let's go back a bit . .

Chapter 3

I'm going to be a Missionary!

When I was nine the teacher in my class read us some of the story of Dr David Livingstone and his exploring and bringing healing to whole swathes of central Africa that before that time were totally unknown to the western world. That was it! From that day on I knew what I was going to be - a medical missionary!

Years later those A-level results came with insufficient grades! Despair. What to do? I was in a tight corner. No alternative but to listen to my father. 'Go and re-sit them!' I'd lost my place at medical school in London for the next year. I'd just finished the residential training course and was waiting, any day, for my ticket to fly off, to what is now Lesotho, in central South Africa, to teach for a year, in a school up in the mountains with Voluntary Service Overseas. It was going to be a great experience, a great adventure. Now all expectations were dashed. I was totally gutted. The feelings. The film easily re-runs in my minds' eye. It was a drizzly late summers day, as I walked aimlessly towards the city, bawling my eyes out, screaming at God - out loud, caring nothing of who might hear. Literally, my world had crashed to the ground. God why have you done this! Great sobs and agony I'd never experienced before.

Worse still, I knew it - of course, I was a failure! I deserved it. Despair was appropriate. I'd not given myself enough to my studies. I'd spent far too much time and energy at school those last years as a boarder, leading the school CCF as senior under officer, managing one of the boarding houses as House Captain, then Head of House, while at the same time leading the Christian rock band. I was being me. I loved it. The state I was now in was all my fault, a useless failure. Chickens do come home to roost! Looking back I realise I was experiencing, at a point in time, my 'brokenness'. It was a long time before I was able, really able, to embrace this brokenness and experience it being replaced with something so wonderful . . . but that's still to come, I still must not rush ahead too fast.

No other choice. Another A-Level year. This time at Medway College of Technology. A small science A-Level course amongst thousands of day release students. I submitted with just two of those wretched A-levels to improve this time! Africa and Medical School were absolutely a thing of the past now, and I really knew it. Maybe God must have something else for me.

At least there was a Christian Union that met in the lunch hour at Medway Tech, at most ten students. One an enthusiastic 'black-n-white' Pentecostal! Very pushy 'You've got to speak in tongues.' What on earth is that? That all finished back then! I checked it out with my dad - 'absolutely not' - the Holy Spirit came at conversion and 'tongues' finished with the early church. Sorted, I'd got that one straight.

It turned out however to be a game-changer of a year and so worthwhile. I became a part of the large and lively Youth Group in the Canterbury Baptist Church. Oh yes, by the way, I happened on my first girlfriend. Summer came - a Summer Crusade in France with a relatively new and totally radical mission group, Operation Mobilisation, as a result of their rep who'd visited the College CU. That summer I learnt so much about hands-on evangelism, Christian literature, denying self, and witnessing so much passion for Jesus. My horizons were being blown wide open. A bonus arrived in the post, the right grades came through!

Three months later I was helping as a volunteer in the Baptist Church Youth Centre in Moss Side, Manchester. It was a tough deprived area at that time. There had been a recent massive influx of immigrants from the West Indies, what came to be known as the Windrush Generation. I was in a totally different culture of learning and relating to people I'd never been exposed to before.

College Days

Moving on twelve months I was starting a four-year theological course training for ministry in Baptist churches. So much had changed to get me this far. Wow! God had dramatically spoken, and opened doors. What a turnaround in my heart and expectations.

I could never have guessed what happened over the next four years. I was surprised and challenged to the very depths of my being. New things were happening all around me. What came to be called the charismatic movement was growing up and down the country and also round the world. It was definitely happening in the Kent town where my parents were. My father came home from working in the City one evening telling of how God had healed his eyes that day. He'd been prayed for at a lunch time meeting he'd attended. Walking to the station along Wigmore Street after the meeting he'd seen a dustbin at the side of the pavement.

He threw his glasses in the bin. He could now see perfectly. Both he and my mother were telling about their experience of the 'Baptism of the Holy Spirit.' They had already been born again Christians for decades. I couldn't dispute that they were now different!

This was during my first term at college. I felt totally isolated. There was not even the slightest hint of any interest in such things in the college, rather I'd picked up the complete opposite from the students in the year above me. Absolute hostility to anything of that kind. It was exactly the same in my year group.

After study finished, at ten in the evenings, bunches of us would get together in our rooms to unwind, drinking coffee and discussing, joking, enjoying time together. All too often it was not unwinding but rather winding up! It turned out to be the issue of the day. 'Did we or did we not receive all of the Holy Spirt at conversion?' 'Did the gifts of the Holy Spirit cease when the New Testament became available?' I was torn between what I was hearing and seeing in my home town and the strong knowledgeable arguments of my fellow students, supported by the teaching of a well loved preacher, who had retired just that year, Dr Martin Lloyd Jones at Westminster Chapel. He had had a significant impact on several students over the years. They were convinced that he taught that it all came at conversion. His 'Banner of Truth' published commentaries on Romans proved the point. Ironically, it wasn't until some years later that it became clear that the publishing house had edited out all reference to such things because they did not agree with such theology and practice. Rather, Martin Lloyd-Jones had encouraged the baptism of the spirit and availability of the gifts of the Holy Spirit over his many years at Westminster Chapel!

I was caught in the middle. On one hand what seemed to be a powerful argument based on scripture and the practice of generations, and on the other, a growing experience across all denominations of so many people finding a new reality and experience with Jesus and healing in their lives. Praise and worship, transformed lives and a whole new vibrance was everywhere.

I read and re-read the Acts of the Apostles, I earnestly sought God and prayed into the night in my college room. I asked, begged, fasted, pleaded if this is right, please do it for me. I knew it was for me, but I was just not experiencing it!

At the start of my second term I had a conversation with one of my year. Malcolm had been as 'flaky as a Cadbury's Flake' in his first term. Over the Christmas vacation he had been turned upside down and inside out! He came back to College a different person entirely. He and his new girlfriend had both had a radical transformational experience of Jesus through the Holy Spirit. At a meeting in a solicitor's office in central London, one Sunday morning, along with hoards of other people, Malcolm and Lyndsey, who was the new girl friend, had been baptised with the Holy Spirit and were now speaking in tongues! But more than that, to my great surprise and delight I discovered that half of the students at the College, now in their third and fourth years, had also had similar experiences the previous year. Due to the ructions caused by one of the students stepping over the line, with an inappropriate 'word of prophecy,' for the College Principal, this student had been immediately expelled; consequently all such things had gone underground.

Towards the end of my second term I was back at home for the weekend. My parents were hosting a meeting - an ex-missionary was speaking about receiving the Holy Spirit. I meant business, so I went for prayer to receive the Spirit at the conclusion of the meeting with one other person. This 'one other' had been my first ever girl friend. I'd 'ditched' her a year or so before when I went off to college!

In a separate room the visiting speaker prayed for the young lady to receive the Holy Spirit first - she came out beaming, floating on air! Then my turn. I really believed and was desperate - but I didn't feel anything. Instead that night I was fighting feelings of great disappointment. Yet again - 'why can't I be like everyone else?' However, I had another thought, a response, 'Thank you Jesus! Thank you for giving me your Holy Spirit just as I need. It's your promise, I will believe it! Help my unbelief!'

Eric, the speaker from the evening before, had been staying the night at my parents' house and came down to breakfast the next morning. He was due to speak in a nearby town at another house meeting that morning and said he had something to share with me and the lady he'd also prayed for that previous night. My mother came up with a great idea, wink, wink. 'Barry can use my car to drive you to your meeting and pick up the young lady on the way.'

And so it happened. After the meeting, now in the house owner's study, Eric presented us both with a shocking prophetic insight. He knew nothing about either   of us, or our past. 'God intends you both to serve him together!' As I walked out I remember my response to Sue: 'Well, we'll see about that! Ok, maybe we need to meet up sometime.' That weekend turned out to be a very special one, with significant life changing effect.

Chapter 4

Launching Out
Tasting the First Fruit

As my first year at college came to an end there were opportunities to get out to the churches, many of which had outreach missions into their areas during the summer break. I'd been invited with several others from my year to make up a team on an outreach with a Baptist church into their city in the south west of England. The team was led by a college student in the year above us.

On the first evening the church was gathered in the church hall and we were all we seated around tables with coffees, teas and cakes. There was an impressive number of church people. It was an opportunity to meet the student team. We were to introduce ourselves one at a time and say something about becoming a Christian and about ourselves. The team members took their turns covering how they'd come to Jesus and why they were at Spurgeon's College. For my turn, in all innocence, I said that I'd known Jesus from and early age through the influence of Christian parents and then I said that this had been a special year for me being baptised in the Holy Spirit that Easter. I was expressing what had become a growing conviction in me over the previous months since that Easter. I knew I had to exercise faith in relation to what I had asked God for that night when I'd been prayed for, and was certain he would make it real for me in the way that he wanted.

What a watershed evening that turned out to be for me in that church hall in Exeter! The first part came immediately after the meeting ended. The team leader took me into a side room and in the strongest, most vehement language possible he demanded, 'Never say anything like that again here. If you can't agree to that you go home right now!' He then sought to justify his outburst by saying that the baptism of the Holy Spirt had caused great trouble in that church in the recent past.

The second watershed was ready to cascade. I went back to my hosts' home that first night with my tail between my legs, feeling totally wasted. I put on my best smiley face possible with my friendly hosts, then escaped to my room and fell on my face before my heavenly Father and wept, quietly. Strange to say it was a turning point for me. That night I experienced my heavenly Father in a whole new way. There was no shame, nor feeling a failure. My weeping changed from feeling useless to tears of joy with freedom and acceptance by Jesus and my Father. I'd come out! After all these months He'd been waiting for me to come to Him, and trust Him, for what was going to be real for me - not hankering after someone else's experience.

A Profound Experience

My relationship with Jesus and his Father was being made real by His Holy Spirit as I walked by faith. Boom! The sun of His presence was breaking through like I'd never experienced before. Really learning the significance of faith demanding me to trust God and his Word was to be put to the test and proved so much in the days and years ahead.

The reality of this faith is a million miles from the fluffy wishful hopefulness so often espoused! Without us actively choosing and acting upon our trust in Him, we remain disappointed.

What Provision!

It was two years to the month after that intervention by my heavenly Father, that Sue and I got married. By now Sue was in her second year as a student nurse at Kings College Hospital in Camberwell, South London and I was in my third year at college - both of us had a year to qualify. The previous two years Sue and I had travelled a million miles in our relationship together. Repentance on my part for the way I'd treated her, when I broke up our relationship those years before, was made easy by the gracious and gentle heart of Sue. We took it slowly and carefully; the journey was wonderful. God's hand on it all was glorious. There was absolutely no doubt that we were meant for each other. Sue was so good for me and a wonderful divine gift, demonstrated in all the ups and downs of our journey together, over the next decades. Sue, what a very special lady!

Before our wedding we had both agreed that our heavenly Father would have to provide a home and the money we would be needing. Sue was now getting paid a small amount and I was still just a student with no income.

Somehow, I had a conversation with Walter Mackie, a fellow student at college. Walter was definitely a 'mature student.' He was taking a year out from teaching in a secondary school on the Stockwell Road, in order to refresh his ministry as the pastor of the small Baptist church in Camberwell. When he heard of my engagement to Sue and her working on Denmark Hill at the hospital, completely out of the blue, he told me there was accommodation at the front of their church building, just off Camberwell Green; it hadn't been occupied for a while and the rent wouldn't be very high as it would be good to just have it used again.

I restrained myself from snapping his hand off on the spot. We agreed Sue and I should go and give it the once over. It would only be a short walk to the hospital and for me it was on the main bus route to South Norwood Hill where the college was.

The day arrived and we knocked on the door. Apologetically, Walter let us in. He explained that it had been the Salvation Army Hall at the back with the frontage being Officers' accommodation. A few years before, the Salvation Army had heard that the large Baptist church building across the road had to be demolished due to safety concerns, and they had given their hall to the Baptist church as they no longer used it.

When the Baptists took the building over, the small house at the front had been occupied, but that came to an end some time before. All the windows at the front were covered with corrugated iron sheets, with the broken glass from the windows scattered on the ground below.

We went inside. There was a kitchen with a sink and a gas point for a cooker along with a living room downstairs. Next to the stairs was a door with a step down to the bath, a sink and another door to the outside. This whole space obviously ran down the side of the meeting hall and on the other side was the boundary wall of the adjacent petrol station. Ten yards down the side of the walkway was another door, to the outside toilet. The walkway was a bit draughty due to the shattered corrugated plastic roof that was scattered on the floor. Upstairs, via the very rickety staircase, were three small rooms.

Yes, it obviously needed a bit of attention, re-roofing the outside walkway to the toilet, the damp and collapsed plaster on the bathroom's outer wall, carpets, along with redecoration throughout and all the shattered windows re-glazed. But these were all mere details. We thanked Walter and said good bye: Sue and I were in no doubt, this was our Fathers' provision. Thank you Jesus. It just has to be of you! But how much was the rent to be, could we afford it?

Monday came and the students were back for lunchtime, having been all over the place preaching in churches on the Sunday. I told Walter that we'd love to have the use of the property. How much for the rent? Five shillings a week he said. Five shillings! No way, I laughed. We couldn't in all conscience take it for that! We agreed ten shillings a week. Even that was an amazing provision for us. For those of you modern people, ten shillings became fifty pence the next year, when decimalisation came in! We had expected to have to pay at least five pounds in the old money.

We had a plan over the next month before we got married: to re-decorate and do the repairs and then when we got back from honeymoon I'd strip off the corrugated iron from the windows and reglaze. We couldn't do that before we moved in, as the windows would all get smashed again.

That's the way it all wonderfully fitted together. We were given a second hand gas cooker and all the furniture we needed. With the decorating done, replacing the roofing on the side walkway and the bathroom wall covered with plywood to cover up the damp, the whole place was transformed. 'What a trust worthy heavenly Father you are!' Such a dramatic lesson in trust this had all been! There was so much more yet to learn, as testing times lay ahead. But little did we know at that time of this 'walk of faith.

Chapter 5

Discovering a Wonderful Gift - Emotion

Those Formative Early Years

Our very early years so often have a profound and lasting effect on us, how we are shaped, think and behave.

My mother's father and mother were a massive part of my early years. They always lived close by. When we as a family moved, grandparents also moved. They had just one child that survived birthing and for most of those years, as my grandfather was retired, they were free to stay close to their daughter, our Mum.

At a young age you don't question things, it's the way they are, so you accept and fit in. Only as my teen years progressed did I become increasingly aware of how it had been. There was a fixed routine all those years. Monday afternoons our mother would take us to visit the grandparents and mother would sit and chat with her mother. Wednesday afternoons grandmother would visit us for the afternoon. Grandfather who was called Bert, would drive and drop her off before returning at six o'clock for the return trip. On very special occasions my brother and I would stay over with the grandparents, in their bungalow. When our sister was born we had to stay for ten days and then for two weeks the time our parents went for a get away to Scotland.

For me the experience was scary; there was something about the bungalow, and it was even worse at night. There was that scary tick-tock of the old grandfather clock just outside our bedroom door. Having to share the small double bed with my brother certainly didn't make the whole stay any better!

Monday afternoon visits every week were also strange. I was learning. Their bungalow always seemed dark. Sometimes frightening for a six year old. One summer day I came back into the house from playing in the garden. The adults were sitting drinking tea. The breeze caught the door behind me with a bang. My grandfather jumped out of his seat, hands to his ears, 'Oh my God! You creature!' he screeched at me, to my terror. What had I done?

My grandmother rarely left the house; husband Bert always did the shopping. On special occasions he would take her in the car for a ride, later when they moved to the coast, to the esplanade.

Grandfather was an able pianist and took great pride in his shiny black baby grand piano. I remember times when he played and encouraged my older brother, who was getting into piano playing himself.

On one occasion I remember coming into the room and grandfather was playing excellent flowing tunes till he came to a halt, bent over the keyboard sobbing, with tears running down his face, he seemed heart broken. He closed the keyboard lid, stood and left the room apologising to what seemed like strong disapproval from his wife with, 'Oh Bert!' in her strong Scottish accent. I didn't know what to make of it all. That was the last time I ever heard my grandfather play his piano. Some emotional switch had obviously been thrown.

Through the years I learnt that lesson. Emotion is bad! Showing emotion is a sign of weakness. Ok, laughing is all right, you can have that; make jokes, 'pull the leg;' but crying in public, sobbing at a sad TV film - no way. In so many ways I had it imprinted in me. The only times I saw emotion expressed in any way between my grandparents was with intense disapproval.

In my own home I was learning the same lesson. My mother evidently had emotions. Dad's responses endorsed the obvious, emotion must be controlled and not expressed.

Those years when we lived in Grays Lane I remember watching when Mum was struggling at the dinner table; something was causing her pain as she sobbed. Dad would come over and stroke her on the arm and say 'there there, there there, love,' obviously trying to make it go away. Expressing emotion was so obviously a significant weakness, to be controlled and denied any expression. There it was again; emotion is bad!

Another one of those really early memories, is when I was sitting in my high chair at the table holding my mother's hand, crying. Some years later on many occasions when we were living in Ashtead, I must have been between six and nine years old, I would again stretch out my hand during the meal, hold her hand and just sob! I don't remember having done something wrong beforehand or feeling unhappy at all. My mum held my hand and I felt her smile. It was so good. However, around the table I picked up the strange looks, brother to father, father to mother with raised eyebrows and mother's knowing smile in reply. But I was not bothered, I felt so good, sobbing and smiling, feeling that warm hand in mine. Why would I remember these experiences when I was so young? What was all that about? Yet much of my teenage experience was so harsh.

Was Jesus Emotional?

What a fascinating man Jesus was when he lived on earth! Three of the writers of the New Testament gospels lived, walked, talked, observed, questioned and discussed with Jesus. Mark wrote the second Gospel as his close friend, the apostle Peter, dictated his close personal experiences of Jesus to him. All four Gospel records are quite clear: Jesus, the very Son of God, gave up all his heavenly rights and lived among his disciples, one hundred percent a human!

So many examples are given, and all four writers build the self same picture - Jesus in his humanity had feelings. Jesus experienced disappointment and intense let downs. The way Jesus looked at Peter on that fateful night, with such a heart of compassion. Peter was utterly broken inside having just denied knowing Jesus.

Jesus demonstrated that he had deep feelings for ordinary people. Examples are recorded so many times. He realised that those 5,000 men women and children were hungry at the end of a long day of his sharing words of life with them. He knew what they needed, not just the spiritual bread, 'We must feed these thousands of men women and children!'

Everything about Jesus demonstrated it - he had feelings. Not only did Jesus have emotions but he engaged with them and was not ashamed of expressing them. His close friend Lazarus, whom he loved was dead. Jesus wept, publicly! Jesus knew times of deepest, darkest anguish that dark night, agonising alone with his Father in the Garden of Gethsemane for hours; the prospect of being separated for the first time ever, from his Father; experiencing such immense emotional pain, expressed through his body sweating blood. Totally incomprehensible.

Then going through the most horrendous physical, mental and emotional suffering through hours of torture nailed to a wooden cross, to finally cry out: 'Father, Father. Why have you forsaken me.'

Emotions are a wonderful gift that take us to a whole new level of relationship. Jesus knew this was a gift he had from his Father. Wonderfully Jesus fulfilled his role and responsibility. The way Jesus lived, taught and died pointed and demonstrated what his Father, the creator of all things, is like.

God the Father too!

Yes, it is true our Heavenly Father is emotional! He is the source of all things, 'nothing is apart from Him.' The reason he could give this wonderful gift to humankind is because it is a part of him. To be specific, God feels joy and God feels sadness. Our heavenly Father, the source of our life, is emotional! It's part of who he is. He feels emotions. They are a part of his nature in a consummate, perfect way.

The Apostle Paul in the first chapter of his letter to the Colossian church writes connecting Jesus inseparably, identically, to God the Father. 'He (Jesus) is the image of the invisible God, the firstborn of all creation' (Col 1:15). Jesus, during his three year ministry demonstrated emotion in so many ways reflecting the Father, absolutely.

I find this truly revolutionary and profoundly liberating. Despite what my background and upbringing may say and, maybe yours, that emotion and showing emotion is bad, to be denied and ashamed of - (except on the terraces of football matches and in certain other socially acceptable occasions!) Our Creator says otherwise, demonstrated by his Messenger in ways that we can all relate to. However it must also be added that, as with all the wonderful gifts that God has given to humanity, emotion can be expressed for good or ill!

Family Legacy Lingers

I've come to recognise the world both my father and mother were born into. They were children of a different age with a different culture. The previous century still believed in the age of chivalry and the glory of advancing into battle mounted on your noble steed, wielding your sword or lance, wearing a shiny helmet with its fine coloured plume. To die in battle for your country was the noblest of ends. Gallantry.

When decisions were taken by those in power, seated in their comfortable clubs, confident that their victory goals would be realised in a couple of weeks, the stiff upper lip prevailed; any sign of emotion was shame. Emotion was reprehensible!

Raised and living in South Africa, my mother's father signed up as a young man to fight the Germans in German West Africa. This was just a precursor to what came to be known months later as The Great War. Rather than a quick victory to the allies, all over in a few weeks, as was promised, history tells a different story of the next five years. So many thousands of lives lost in unspeakable circumstances. The long term effects, on those left at home and those fortunate to be able to return, was indelibly imprinted on their generation and the generation to come. My mother's father, my grandfather, was one of those.

Grandad survived by a miracle. Going 'over the top' seeking to advance on the German lines across 'no man's land', he was hit by the onslaught of German shells. Unconscious, he fell to the ground with part of his guts blown out. He fell into one of the thousands of deep water-filled shell craters. In his unconscious state he miraculously fell onto a plank of wood stretching across part of the water, inviting his death.

The attack failed and what was left of his platoon retreated, taking such bodies as they could. Bert was still breathing. He survived, leaving part of his intestines behind. Eventually repatriated to his Scottish regiment's home in Scotland. Following surgery and after many months, he recovered. However, he never recovered from the overwhelming 'shell shock' as it was called at that time. Both he and his nurse, whom he eventually married, never recovered from the profound experience of that time. Any form of emotion had to be repressed. It seemed to be the only way to survive life, but at what a cost?

This was the environment my mother was brought up in. The slightest banging noise and her father went ballistic - fierce language with a powerful effect. Then, add to this, something I had learnt late in my teen years; my mother had been one of twins. At child birth, her mother experienced prolonged desperation, physical agony and profound mental repercussions when the second child was finally still born. Like many who went through those war times, God was blamed and hated. And then there was all the pain and anxiety of living through the London Blitz of the Second World War.

My father's family history was different but with a similar effect. His father and uncle survived the First World

War and the family building business thrived - until the financial 'crash' at the end of the 1920s. Some decades earlier the family's move from Lancashire to prosperous Surrey was a smart move and greater prosperity followed. They were definitely 'well to do.' Children in private schools and only greater good things to come.

The disastrous 'crash' came in 1928. The building industry so often being one of the first to feel the pinch. Loyal staff were laid off with no State assistance at that time. The pressures were growing and the business' future was dire. Uncle could bear it no longer. He jumped in front of a train at Wimbledon Station. This uncle's brother was my father's father, who now was left holding the baby. He struggled on with the business for a few more years doing the best he could but liquidation was coming. The pressure was evidently too great and he had a cerebral aneurysm and died. With no more business, my father, at sixteen, was now responsible for his mother and young sister; there was no National Health Service or State Benefit in those days. There was no alternative for my father; he gave up his dreams and prospects, he had to find work and provide food for mother and sister. He faced up to it and got a job in a winding factory making electrical transformers.

In three years he signed up with the army. War had again been declared. World War II, just twenty years on from the last one. My father, Norman, did well. He was earning some money to send to his family. He progressed in officers' training and off he went - for the next six years. He served on many continents, rose through the ranks to Major and in the middle of his time was married to Myrtle, my mother. Time in Burma, experiencing the expansion of the Japanese through that region; England and preparations for

'D Day,' followed by harrowing sights and sounds on and after the Normandy landings only to be trapped in the Falaise Gap for three months before the allies could break out and proceed towards Germany. After this he was posted to India, assigned to the Police service as they prepared for independence from Great Britain in 1947.

During his time in India, back home, his wife bore their first child, my brother David, the same year the war in Europe ended, 1945. Though the British troops were 'de-mobbed' and sent home, Norman was ordered to stay and see his responsibilities through with the Indian Government. Nearly two years later, he, too was 'de-mobbed' and finally sailed back home, seeking to adjust to civvy street, to find a job to support his family and, like so many others, having no qualifications. Getting reacquainted with his wife and meeting a son for the first time, who had bonded with his grandfather in his father's absence. Challenging times. While underneath the surface dealing with the horrors he'd witnessed first hand; coping with the awesome fears when crossing the rough English Channel seas followed by the horrendous sights following the Normandy landing. Then the night dreads, stuck in India and never getting back to see his wife and new son. It was many decades before post traumatic stress disorder (PTSD) was recognised.

And what about all that my mother must have gone through - never spoken about? What if he never came back? What if she had to raise her son all on her own? What if she was never going to be able to be loved by the man she had spent so little time with over the previous five years? What to do with all those deep feelings of love, hope, expectation, anger and fear? But not just for her but for her young son?

44

How do you live with the prospect of being one of those 'war widows'?

There was only one way, the safe way. Shut down the feelings. Give the emotions and feelings space and they just weaken you, make you feel a failure, less than a proper father or mother and, of course, what would the effect be on the poor child? Be strong. Deny the emotions. And they did. They had to.

I have come to realise and appreciate the significance and the power of the cultures my parents and their parents were born into. How it shaped them and then all they had to face and come through. What damage and what a price to pay.

I am in no doubt at all. Both my parents were truly emotional people and, of course, had feelings. Quite understandably, theirs was the culture that shaped my early years. Now the fifties ushered in an age of radical cultural change. The 'swinging sixties' were here and I was heading into my teen years. Change was here and here to stay. Everything was changing. It seemed as if nothing now was off limits. Attitudes to feelings, emotion and 'experience' were centre stage.

Wonderfully, our gracious Father God, was also profoundly at work. He was sowing seeds even then; watering those seeds of experiencing an intimate God, connecting and bringing release to our feelings, emotions and experience of him and our fellow human beings, was on the way. Over the next decades so much changed. This teenager had a long journey ahead to begin to accept what was so natural for him and so near the surface, to freely experience this wonderful God-given Gift.

As for my mum and dad to this day I am so sad that they never were able to realise and come to terms with this wonderful gift that God had created and had gifted them with. So sad that neither of them were able to come to a place of the full freedom God created them for.

Wendy Mann tells her story in her book 'Leading As Sons and Daughters.' As a result of God's dealing in her life she says:

'Although I still have more to learn about being emotionally healthy, I am in a completely different place now to where I used to be. My heart feels more alive than ever, I can feel deep pain and grief but also overwhelming joy. The wonderful thing about this transformation is the legacy I now get to leave. One of my strengths when I travel around speaking at other churches is giving people permission to feel and express emotion.' (Leading As Sons and Daughters. Page 175 Malcolm Down Publishing. 2019)

I'm now convinced; emotion is indeed a wonderful God-given Gift; with a purpose.

Chapter 6

A Discipline with Lasting Benefit

During the year before College I'd come across something that seemed a good idea. It seemed quite novel and I decided to give it a try. It would definitely make a difference to an area that I felt was a great weakness.   I signed up and received in the post the first stage of my TMS kit! The Topical Memory System from the Navigators. The way it worked was a different Bible verse with the reference, to be memorised each day. Stage one was a series of related topics. Each day there was a little card, with the chapter and the verse and the reference repeated at the end. The discipline was to say the reference, the text, then the reference over and over. The card fitted into a little flip open closed holder with a special space showing just the reference. The idea was to look at the card while learning, then test oneself seeing only the reference. As each day of the week progressed you added the next card, then tested yourself on the previous cards that week. When you reached the end of the week, you tested yourself on all seven - only seeing the references.

The amazing thing was that it worked! The first series were basic gospel verses pointing to how to become a Christian. The following series moved on to walking in the

Christian life. I think something must have been realised by my parents, hearing me chanting Bible verses from my bedroom. I thought I'd explain, a few weeks into it; my father had never heard of such a thing but seemed to listen with interest. To my great surprise a few weeks later dad had his Topical Memory System and was likewise enthusiastically bitten! I never dreamt that he would have needed it. What a wonderful blessing that daily discipline proved to be, as stage went on to stage and one dozen verses lead to many dozens.

It could however, seem a bit weird. Later Sue and I were in our first year of marriage and for part of the long summer vacation I got a job at Peak Freans Biscuit factory in Bermondsey, a short ride on my Honda 90. I was put on the bourbon and custard cream production lines. My job was to go up and down the two long conveyer belt lines collecting, then emptying, the boxes of broken and discarded biscuits from the workers along the lines. It was tedious work, forever walking up and down the lines at least 150 yards long; definitely keeping me fit and then relieved with the break - opportunity to sit down! TMS was also a good opportunity to focus my mind on the Good News, during the boring work routine.

One day I noticed some of the girls, on one of the lines, tittering among themselves then looking up at me as I walked past. What had I done now? I stopped alongside them to increased laughter and one said, 'Is this yours?' while holding up one of my TMS cards. 'You dropped it when you walked past earlier; we thought it was yours.' I thanked them with a smile as they handed me the card and I added, 'I'm a Christian and I'm learning Bible verses.' Those in hearing range laughed out loud. As I walked away,

I smiled to myself and thought, 'At least they know that now.'

To this day I've no regrets about the time and effort invested in the Topical Memory System and dad definitely became an enthusiast. I've checked and fifty years on it's still available - I guess that says something! Yes, why not give it a try?

Chapter 7

A Significant Discovery

South Oxley Student Pastor

Part of the college ministerial training offered the option of twelve months 'doing the job' as a student pastor. As my first college year was ending, a fellow student in the year ahead of me, approached me. His year as a student pastor was coming to an end, so would I take over his student pastorate? It was a small Baptist church on a council estate north of London in Hertfordshire. He'd enjoyed his year and thought that I'd do a good job. He said it wasn't too onerous. It had to fit alongside all the other aspects of continuing the college and degree course and all the other activities, but you only had to be there every other week for a long weekend and as long as you liked during vacation time. Sounded to me like an opportunity. I agreed to go and speak there and then the church could decide, Yay or Nay!

I did it. I waited to hear the result with a bit of trepidation. After John, the current student pastor, had visited the next week, I waited to hear the result. I was prepared for it to go either way. Monday afternoon after that weekend everyone was back in college from their various preaching engagements. John gave me the thumbs up saying they would have me. They didn't really have any other choice. It was a small regular congregation of about three dozen. There was a very committed core of folks and they were going for it. It had been much larger, but times had changed. However, there was an active Sunday School with a great leader, and what turned out to be a a good bunch of teens who got together

on a Friday night. A real surprise was the sizeable Boys Brigade that met mid-week. Interestingly, the main leader and most of the boys never came to the Sunday services but lived on the estate, South Oxhey, just outside of Watford.

It was the year before Sue and I were married and I relished the experience and learned so much while I was the student pastor of that North London church. I was beginning to discover what I was good at - I did well with people. It was challenging, invigorating, and relationships were working. I loved it though not all were easy. I felt I was connecting with me!

Year Four - The Final Year

Eventually came the final college year; hours of hard graft preparing for the final university exams and supporting Sue as she finished her nurses training, while now based in our first home - the tiny house in a rough, tough, area of Camberwell Green.

But there was a puzzling problem. As the end of the four years approached all my contemporaries had been out 'preaching with a view,' trying out and being tried out at Baptist churches that needed a new minister.

Sometimes the minister was also called the pastor. He was the one in charge. The deacons were selected by the votes of the church members. The minister did the rest. The most sought after ministers were those that excelled at preaching. The students that were good at teaching were

51

snapped up quickly. I was in a turmoil. Surely, so many of those around me were not really 'pastors'? And they also had to be lots of other things - truly gifted, teachers, good managers, enthusiastic for ministry and had all completed the college pastoralia classes, learning how better to fill the role demanded. For the next few decades I had a growing strong aversion to the term pastor. If that is what a pastor is that's certainly not me!

However, towards the end of my last summer term, having no other direction from God, I gave in and went to 'preach with a view' at an inner London church near to where we lived. The Sunday morning came, I walked up the steps to the main entrance to be greeted at the door by the church secretary. 'By the way, the person who visited us recently has just got back to us and accepted our invitation to be our next minister'. 'No problem at all' I replied. A huge weight lifted as I walked into the church building and served them as best I could for morning and evening services.

The relief and sense of freedom I felt was enormous. Now I'm certain. There's no doubt. This is not where I fit! It's not what God has for me.

The reason I didn't feel I fitted was because it was not me. God my Father knew what He'd created me for. I wasn't walking away from church. There just had to be more - it was not the same as all that I'd been seeing in the early church and was getting more excited about over those past four years. All I knew was that I did not fit. He was calling me and Sue for something else!

Chapter 8

Another Powerful Discovery

The Power of Listening

When the last exam finished my time was up. One thing remained, I'd taken the option of a two week 'Clinical Theology Course' at a North London Mental Hospital. The afternoon we arrived, me and eight others, from different London theological colleges, sat down in the office of the two hospital chaplains. We sat in a circle around the desk. They started with words of welcome. Then . . . . nothing. Silence. Silence which continued, to the growing embarrassment and puzzlement of us students. After what seemed an eternity, one of the students blurted out and started talking about himself. Someone else followed. Followed by more silence.

What sort of course is this? I felt offended the way these leaders were just sitting there, saying nothing. It was embarrassing. Rude. This is not the way to behave; we've come to learn about care and how to cope with people with severe psychiatric issues. Out of frustration I wanted to speak out, break the silence and get on with it. I looked round at the other students, they were experiencing the same embarrassed silence. I bit my tongue.

But a whole new training had started. It was an object lesson of how we should relate to the patients that we would be spending most of our time with during the weeks ahead: 'shut up and listen.' As the days went by, when we met in the mornings for our daily meeting, they always started the same way, but gradually changed. The students began to talk. We all listened. It was different. I for my part was beginning to get it! 'Shut up Barry, and intentionally listen to the person.' I began to put it into practice as I built one-on-one relations with the patients.

I didn't have answers to what I was being confronted with; men and women living under lock and key. All I could do was listen. Wow, this is different. I was learning so much. Listen - stop talking! Relate!

After the six weeks; I came away with those two things that were to become a part of me, 'Shut up and listen.'

A significant part of college training had been emphasising the centrality of teaching in church life, reaching the lost, doing the work of ministry, taking the initiative, leading, directing the deacons and demonstrating a strong headship in the church. This demanded that 'we' do the talking! We've had the training, we know the Bible, can quote the proper meaning of the Greek words, and maybe the Hebrew as well. The powerful expectation is that the minster, pastor or preacher will perform, the ones that do it best, are highly acclaimed and definitely the most desired. I bought into it; it's what I expected of myself; they had been shaping me. Eventually I began to see the truth of it and I was seeing how these expectations can become very harsh task masters - as they are for us all.

What a disappointment Jesus was for so many people when he started his three years of ministry. So many years and centuries waiting and longing for the Messiah, and now he's come. But this was not what they expected, not like this Jesus.

With His disciples, over the years, Jesus got to know them intimately, in part by listening to their conversations as they sat together, walked from town to town, when they discussed things that were happening. Seeing how they had been shocked at some of the miracles he'd done; listening to the people's responses and their own fears and successes. We have so many examples of when Jesus intentionally taught the crowd and individuals and commented on what was happening around him. But this was just a part of how Jesus related. He also listened.

Jesus listened at different levels. He heard the words. He listened to the person speaking, the whole person, what they were expressing with body language, their facial language, tone of voice, and, something even more profound and revealing, Jesus listened to people's hearts. Time and again we have example of this in the gospel records. When he had conversations with folk Jesus 'saw into their hearts' connecting to their true underlying feelings, needs and attitudes. So often his responses to people seemed to have no connection to what they had said, yet were so revealing and opened doors to expose their real needs - then offering answers.

There is a simple response to this. 'This is Jesus, Son of God, he is different to me.' But wait a minute. Jesus on this earth was 100% human and lived and died totally human. Like us in every way! Listening to people, for us too, can be so much more than just hearing the words that they say. So often people will tell us so much about themselves and be so vulnerable with us, if we will but listen. Just as a truly productive apple tree takes years to transform from a sapling into an array of mature branches with dozens of inviting, crisp, sweet, ripe apples, so our gracious heavenly Father carefully nurtures and disciplines his dear children! So he's been with me. I've been such a slow learner.

The Question

After that Clinical Theology Course that summer, while Sue was in her last six months of training, I had the summer free. I was meeting, starting to listen and engaging with people out on the streets of London. I quickly saw the significance of looking for their engagement, before they dismissed me as a total religious nutcase, especially with those tracts in my hand. The most positive way in was to ask them a question right off. Then listen! Most people love to talk about themselves and their opinions, given the opportunity. I was beginning to get it! If the first question doesn't spark, then ask another. Sooner or later, nine times out of ten, they would share surprisingly, telling things about themselves, and so often I had the opportunity of relating the words, actions, relevance of who Jesus is, why he died and why he is alive right now!

It's just the same in a Christian context talking to followers of Jesus. When we 'shock' Christian people by asking them their experiences and opinions, they talk. The starting place I've found to be so important, especially with people I don't know or are meeting for the first time, is not a blunt 'straight to the point' question but, a general question. Hopefully a starter. Not challenging or seeming to pry, but rather gently expressing interest in their opinion or thoughts. For instance, 'How are you coping with this freezing weather at the moment?' Or not even a question, rather a statement invoking a response. 'Your little kid seems to be having a great time; he's very adventurous on the slide!'

Then see where it goes. Maybe nowhere, but so often you'll quickly find out if that person is wanting to talk. If they do, listen. It's amazing where it can go! Simply because you were willing to make contact and express interest. All such a rare commodity in our society.

Often we are surprised when other people express interest in us! It opens doors of relationship. Expressing real interest, listening with compassion and genuine interest, giving time, even if only a few minutes, can have a profound effect. Listening with head and heart. Resisting the temptation of solving their problems with our quick words is often hard. So often it's the wisest way to demonstrate genuine interest and care.

We need to face the reality. Such behaviour is counter-cultural. Jesus took seriously teaching his disciples and also the crowds. How many times do we read in the gospel records of Jesus asking questions? Many notable instances come to mind: the Samaritan woman at the well . . . questions to Peter . . . often to his disciples . . . people coming for healing . . . so many.

Chapter 9

Hopelessness

Face to Face

Going back to my time at that psychiatric hospital. As well as the lesson in listening and posing a question, something else was hitting me between the eyes. I felt I was being bombarded; the overall sense of hopelessness was overwhelming, at a deep level, from all the people I was meeting up with, the staff as well! Apart from mixing with the general population, we were allocated a specific person to spend each afternoon with. The more I got to know the young man I had been allocated, the more of the heartbreak I felt. This young man believed he would be locked up there for the rest of his days. We were specifically instructed by the chaplaincy team leading our course that we were not permitted to talk religion to the inmates. Whether that made it easier or harder for me, I don't know. One thing I now know for certain, is that all these decades later, such institutions have changed radically. However, 'Hope deferred makes the heart sick, but a desire fulfilled is a tree of life.' (Proverbs 13:12).

But that was just the beginning back then in the 1970s. Our present age, from cradle to grave, is so full of promise, promises and expectations. From well-meaning parents, and the earliest school days onward, today's subtle and powerful advertising and the absolutely essential social media: 'Dream! You can have your dreams. It's your right!'

As the years progress through adolescence into adulthood, if you're not experiencing and dancing through your dreams realised, it's someones fault; teachers, your parents, your stupid partner. It's people who are responsible for not giving you your due. If not them, it's definitely the government's fault - 'not enough money in the system; they should be held responsible.' Or maybe you believe what you're told - you didn't fight hard enough for your rights. Whatever! The result is the same. Growing despair as the years pass and the body misbehaves and wants to give up. So often expectation turns to hopelessness.

Some have not been so optimistic and by late teens it's all got too much! It's what I encountered in the face, on that clinical theology course all those years ago. But now it's everywhere, all walks of life, in poverty and even with riches, all ages, growing hopelessness and despair.

Wonderfully, there is hope and a certain hope at that. The opportunity of living, demonstrating and pointing to the source of that hope, is even more relevant today. When people are genuinely able to connect with their hopelessness - Jesus is transformational power! Our modern world is gagging, for this sort of hope . . . but I'm jumping ahead too much!

After the weeks in the mental hospital, I said farewell to my four years at college after speech day, taking with me much experience, a half decent Bachelor of Divinity degree, but also many big questions. However, I was now settled with certainty that the expression of 'ministry' as it was at that time, in traditional churches was not for me.

Ever so slowly God was building on the foundations in my life; however, there was still much more demolition to be done. 'So God what have you got for us; Sue and I?'

Chapter 10

Where Now? Next Stop . . . Belgium!

London West End

The summer was now ahead. Freedom! Armed with copies of 'The 4 Spiritual Laws' I headed off for central London; anywhere where there were people. There was so much choice; Hyde Park, Trafalgar Square, Piccadilly Circus. Afternoons and then evenings, when Sue was on late duty.

Putting into practice my 'question and listen' lessons, I went for it. There were so many people who looked free to talk. Armed with a smile and what seemed like a suitable opener, 'You visiting London?' Or, if it looked suitable, 'What do you think of Jesus?' or, 'I'm a follower of Jesus, have you heard about him?' It was great! I found it challenging, but people talked. From a zillion nations, all sorts of backgrounds, all sorts of people, young and old. Many willing to talk - some making it quite clear '. . . . off.'

They were great weeks. Challenging, surprising, stimulating and, sometimes, deep stuff. Evenings were different; much tougher, experiencing the sad side of Soho. But I loved it. This was real people, even if in unreal settings! True, not many made professions of faith, but it was real, challenging and I was connecting to people and learning such a lot. This seemed to be me. 'So, what are you saying to me God?'

Strangely, in Piccadilly Circus especially, time after time, I kept meeting men from Turkey. I already knew about Turkey - a country where at that time there were known to be less than a hundred 'born again' Christians, in very few churches.

Eventually, I put my Heavenly Father 'to the test!' I put out a 'fleece' of what would happen. The next day it did! Over the weeks following, it all began to fit together. I was amazed and excited. It became a conviction. Sue caught it too. 'God wants us to go and plant a church in Turkey!'

A great friend in my time in college had left after two years and had joined a new mission group to plant a church in Portugal. At the same time other teams had also started in three other European countries. I heard that the people leading the mission were praying for a team to plant churches in Turkey. Wow! It was all fitting together. This really seemed for us! Awesome!

Action Stations

All systems are go! By January the next year, Sue graduated as a qualified nurse from Kings Hospital. We had the green light to go.

We packed up and got rid of all our furniture. What we felt we needed was stuffed into our beaten up old mini car and we set off for Suffolk for a month-long training programme, with the others joining the mission.

It was early days in the development of this new mission; there were just four us on the training course. It was very special. We were away from it all, in a large country house lent to us for a few months, at no charge. It was located in the middle of nowhere, towards the East Suffolk coast. The leader and his wife had a lot of missionary experience through the large mission they had been serving with for many years.

The leader had previously been in contact with a Canadian missionary, working with Turkish immigrants in Marseilles, southern France. He had agreed that we could join with him and get some experience with Turks, alongside him. The plan was, for Sue and I to begin to adjust to the Turkish culture and move on in learning the language, prior to our launching into Turkey on our own. It made great sense, definitely this was God's provision for us. The only thing was, this missionary was currently back in his home country, Canada, on furlough with his wife and family. It had been agreed he would write and let us know, via our mission leader, when he had arrived back in Marseilles; this would be about the time our training period was to be completed.

The course was exciting, equipping, and a great learning opportunity. It came to an end. The letter didn't come. We waited a further month. For some reason our mission leader tried but was unable to get in touch with the Canadian missionary. What to do, while we waited even longer? We couldn't stay much longer in our current accommodation. What now? A sensible stop gap was suggested while we waited. An Easter outreach mission was due to start, in a week or so, in the outskirts of Brussels. It was to be based on a Belgium Evangelical Mission church; a large team of students from London Bible College were due to arrive. Sue and I decided it made good sense to join with this team of students and be a part of the mission. Surely that letter would arrive during those two weeks, and off we would go.

The mission turned out to be a great experience, with opportunity to practice our French. Easter passed; still no word at all from Canada! Our mission leader was still not able to make any contact with the missionary from Marseilles. Puzzling! More weeks were passing by. We couldn't stay much longer with the family in Brussels.

'Maybe God intends you to stay in Belgium.' The leader of the Belgium Evangelical Mission said one day. 'There are plenty of openings to lead a church in Belgium.' Without delay he made arrangements for Sue and I to visit and speak in a church one Sunday morning, in the far south of the country. It was a small group and they desperately wanted a pastor to lead them. A couple of new friends came with us. As we drove back later in the day Sue and I were in no doubt; without even discussing it. 'No way! This is not of you God, is it!'

'Free University'

A total change of direction came in the next week or so. Sue and I were both convinced; to plant a church among students in ULB, the 'Free University' in Brussels. To correct any misunderstanding, it wasn't free for the students, but it was the only University in Belgium that was not connected to the Catholic Church - it was 'free thinking.'

The journey was exciting. Sue and I started with a great summer crusade; young people joining us from the UK reaching out to people in Brussels. We were contacting many hundreds of people; so many tourists from across the globe 'doing' Brussels, as well as many French speaking and Flemish speaking Belgians living in the city. At the same time, we were preparing for a team to join us in September to work in the university with the French and Flemish speaking students.

They were two exciting years. We saw some people come to know Jesus and we started to disciple them. The university context was extreme left-wing, anti-God and with a high profile of all shades of Maoism, Marxism, Trotskyism; in fact all shades of Communism. We joined them: We set up a Christian book table next to all theirs, in the university foyer every lunchtime, to present a very striking alternative. The rest of the day was spent talking and relating to students in the restaurants and coffee lounges, the majority of whom had grown up in the predominantly Catholic culture of Belgium and held a very strong aversion to religion.

The five of us made a great team and had an exciting buzz. Friday and Saturday evenings were spent out on the streets of Brussels with the team from Teen Challenge, working from their new coffee bar in the centre of the city.

Wonderful Arrival

There was much excitement during those few concentrated years; not the least was the impending birth of our first child, due the next May. Due to our commitments with the folks in Brussels there was no question of returning to the UK for the birth. We made enquires of how it worked where we were living. Sue would have to go into the local specialist birthing centre, which was just down the main road. After the birth she would have to stay on the ward there for a further week. Then came the other bit. There was a hefty bill to pay. We just didn't have that sort of money.

Our Heavenly Father was going to have to do something fantastic.

A few days later I was sharing the situation we were facing with Johan, one of the students who had given his life to Jesus. His response shocked me. 'You're one of the students at the university aren't you, just like me? As students we get medical care free of charge.' You can imagine my reaction. Wow, what a surprise. At the start of the year all of us had signed up at the uni as 'eleves libres'. We all attended just one course once a week, so we were able to get a Student Card enabling us to be legitimately involved on the campus, hold our book table, come and go, spend hours in the cafeteria and qualify for free medical care!

After Sue had 'served' her week adjusting to our brand new-born child and her body was beginning to recover from the very painful birth, followed by the strict regime of the post natal ward, she was longing to get back to our flat and not having to force down that pint of very brown ale every day! That week came to an end and with great excitement and pride, I walked down the street to take her home along with our cuddly one week old baby, Marc. I showed my Student Card to the receptionist. She responded 'that will be just 100 Belgian francs then,' as she started to write out the receipt - panic! I had no money on me. I had no money at home either. What to do? How could I face Sue - she had already seen me walking down the street from her upstairs window and was expecting me at her door at any minute.

As off hand as possible, I apologised for not having brought my money with me, saying I'll pop back and return in twenty minutes. I walked back home crying out to God in utter desperation; wracking my brains for a solution. I came up with none. Not only had I no money at home but I also knew the rest of team, who lived in another flat across town, had nothing either. When I got back to the flat they had all arrived for lunch and were itching to see the new-born. They asked where Sue was, knowing she was due back that morning. With reluctance I explained the situation. Robert responded with a wide smile. 'My support money arrived this morning.' This money meant a lot to them, for the rent for their apartment. Robert handed me 100 francs. With tears in my eyes I thanked him profusely and said I'd pay him back when I could.

I rushed back to the Maternity. As I walked toward the building Sue was leaning out of the window. I handed over the money went to Sue's room and apologised for being delayed. I didn't let on why; I didn't want to spoil the extra special return home with our precious new treasure. 'Thank you Father, thank you, thank you. Your amazing timing was absolutely spot on.' I sang in my heart as we walked the short way back to our apartment and a whole new life as a family of three. A while later, I shared the reason with Sue for my delay that day. We agreed, once again our Father God had demonstrated how able he is to provide, even if it is at the very last moment!

The summer term was now coming to an end. Some of the students were baptised in water in a large inland lake on the edge of Brussels. It was now holiday time with loads of people enjoying the water sports and the beaches. It was a memorable celebration and certainly turned a few eyes.

Total Shock!

As the university year came to an end, we were transferring our time to focusing on the city centre and the Teen Challenge Coffee Bar we'd been involved in through the winter. Following the success of the summer crusade the previous year with volunteers from the UK, we were planing on developing it for the coming summer. The invitations were getting out to our contacts in the UK and plans were advancing. We had sleeping accommodation arranged for both men and women and the purpose-made literature to use on the streets was ready for the printers.

However, two things were happening at the same time. There was a significant unsettling within the leadership of the mission and our support from the UK was all of a sudden shrinking profoundly. Sadly, our monthly newsletter seemed to be having an adverse effect. Some months before, a couple from one of the team's home church, whom we did not know, were enthusiastic to distribute it for us. It sounded good to have others involved helping us out. I had been writing the copy and sent it to them. For several months we assumed that it had been circulating, but then someone made contact telling us the monthly letter was less than helpful. They sent us a copy of what they had received. Sue and I were totally shocked. Bless their hearts, the couple in the UK distributing it for us, had been re-writing it and the result was disastrous! Most of it made absolute nonsense, it didn't bare any resemblance to what we were doing, nor what I'd written. No wonder good folks felt they could no longer support us in what we were seeking to do. I contacted the couple distributing it for us and said I would take the letter back and send it out ourselves. Financially though it was too late.

At the same time we were shocked to hear that the teams from Portugal, Spain and Italy were winding up and returning to the UK. The mission leadership issue was evidently a significant factor; the whole thing was teetering. Added to all this, our financial situation was now in reality not viable. 'God what are you saying to us?' Our three team members were only with us for one year and would soon be returning home. There would be Sue, me and baby Marc. Eventually we knew what we had to do.

We shared everything with our team. Within the month we all returned to the UK. 'But Heavenly Father what have you got for us now?' We had no idea at all. Sue and I were emotionally scrambled.

Sue and I packed our possessions and our three month old Marc into the old VW Beetle we had been given a year or so before and set off to the ferry at Ostend, with just enough money for the crossing to Pegwell Bay on the massive hovercraft.

Very graciously my parents opened their home in Kent to us. Tails between legs and not a little disillusioned, we began to face a penniless future of question marks. Even harder still, was to live under the cloud of father's unspoken, 'I told you so. Oh Barry!' Once again the sense of failure was tangible. Having no answers and seeing no future, was the absolute hardest of hard. 'God, if we ever needed you, we need you now!' Not to forget the five month old son we were now adapting to, and all under the one roof with my mother and father.

Looking back is so much easier than walking it! Our loving heavenly Father was dealing with us so precisely; every detail with a purpose; every shock was fitting into place in his gracious breaking, expanding, transforming and growing process. Why so? Why does he love us so much to take such action?

Chapter 11

Another New World in Four Months

One thing led to another - absolutely none of it planned or ever dreamt of, by Sue or me.

My brother's bright idea was totally out of my orbit! So why not give it a try? The next week I started exploring the local paper. As a result, I started a summer seasonal job bringing in the barley harvest on a local farm. It was half way through August; the sun shone endlessly and it was a wonderfully invigorating physical experience. The days were filled with physically handling hundreds of straw bales on the now harvested fields, then unloading and stacking them into the massive barn. Six weeks passed; muscles grew that I never realised I had.

Following another search in the local paper a permanent job opened up. I was to be a general farm worker on a mixed farm outside Faversham. A small bungalow on the site went with the job. What a wonderful all round provision. An abnormally wet September lay in front of us. The team was just the farm manager and me. I rapidly learnt so much about sheep, store cattle and field crops. It was great experience and I thoroughly enjoyed what I was learning. Sue was also doing so well making our new home in our little modern bungalow on the site, just two minutes walk away for my lunch break.

To the manager's great disappointment within five months I'd left. Sue and I plus our son Marc, and our four chickens, moved into the farmhouse in South Devon with sole responsibility to look after the small flock of sheep and the rest of the farm, before my brother and parents would be able join us the following year. Far fetched I know - but true!

Chapter 12

The World was Changing
The 'Charismatic Movement'

Separate from the small world of Sue and I, God was moving on a pace.

Back in my student days there had been so much happening with this so called 'Baptism in the Spirit' and what came to be called the 'Charismatic Movement.' The Fountain Trust started by Michael Harper, was gathering large numbers to its Saturday afternoon and evening meetings, in the Metropolitan Tabernacle at the Elephant and Castle in London. It was so different, the massive, packed building; there was singing in tongues with enthusiastic singing and powerful testimony of what God was doing. On one occasion I was significantly impressed with Lauren Cunningham, the visiting speaker. He spent the evening talking about the very early days of 'Youth with a Mission' and the vision God was giving him for the future, which included getting a large ocean going boat, with young volunteers, to take the gospel to unreached countries. It sounded so exciting and radical.

It was wonderful to be living in south London at that time; London was a place where so much was happening.

That summer after I'd finished College the 'Festival of Light' was taking to the streets of central London for a week led by Graham Kendrick, and thousands of Christians were joining in. In the afternoons, a young evangelist, Eric Delve, was encouraging us to be bold and tell people about Jesus out on the streets.

These were the days of 'Flower Power.' Starting in California, the impact was speedily felt in London and the UK, with strange flared trousers, flowery tops, smoking pot - 'cool man' and, seemingly, anything goes; and oh yes, the times were changing with Christianity experiencing profound change in the younger generation. Arthur Blessit was in London at this time carrying his 'huge cross', with a little wheel at the bottom. He had just walked across the States from west to east with his cross and he had hit London and was, of course, introducing us to his little round 'Jesus Loves You' stickers, which were covering central London - on lamp posts, in the Underground and on anything that stood still! With all this happening it didn't seem strange for hundreds of young people to turn out and parade through the streets singing Graham Kendrick's whole new style of worship songs, masses were spreading out across the parks and streets and talking to people about Jesus and inviting everyone to the big meeting in Trafalgar Square on Saturday was easy. It was great! It was revolutionary; it hit the main news of the day and disrupted all the London traffic. This new expression of Christianity was coming to people's attention.

The whole understanding and experience of Christian worship was transforming. Graham Kendrick was so gifted with his lyrics and style of music and was finding wide acceptance through his recordings and concerts.

74

'Anchor Recordings' had been started at that time by Peter Wallis. He was recording on cassette tapes, the medium of the day, the talks and singing at the burgeoning Christian events such as Capel Bible Week. Peter had met up with Dave & Dale Garratt of Scripture in Song in New Zealand and agreed to distribute their cassettes of Bible passages set to music in the UK. They took off! Everywhere you went they became known and were being sung in the times of worship in small prayer meetings and large gatherings. A whole new understanding and experience of praise was beginning to emerge.

Family Changes

It was just at this time that my father was taking early retirement from his executive position in the pharmaceutical company and was now getting to know Peter Wallis who also lived in the same area in Kent. Anchor Recordings was doing very well and Peter needed extra help in the expanding business, especially on the finance side. My father, now retired, started helping him out.

It just so happened that this was the time my parents had a 'vision' cooking and were seeking where to relocate to, in order to walk in this 'vision' God was giving them for their future. Peter introduced dad to his brother, who was Arthur Wallis, well known and respected for his speaking ministry and significant book 'In The Day Of Thy Power,' a book on revival that had stirred many in recent years.

Arthur was involved in encouraging a new church group to get established further, west from his home in Devon. Peter Wallis was also considering paying a visit to Devon with the possibility of re-locating Anchor Recordings there. He and my dad agreed to pay a visit together for a few days. 'You never know, maybe God was in it for us as well' was my father's thinking. Both he and my mother had been wondering about the possibility of a small holding - with the interest they were nurturing in 'self sufficiency', based on the Seymours' best selling book of that name, before the popular BBC TV comedy programme 'The Good Life,' became so popular.

Leading up to this time David, my older brother, had also experienced a few years of radical changes. After quite a few years of successful teaching in schools in Northern Ireland, he'd joined the Army and ended up teaching Junior Leaders. However, this new context didn't satisfy him and he decided on a really profound change of career. He got a place back in Kent in a prestigious agricultural and horticultural college for a one year course. However, before he could start the course he needed some months of practical experience - hence six months working on a pig farm.

Big change for David was not over. David had met a very special lady and within a year he was married to Maggie. Maggie had to be a special lady to put up with her new husband's very disgusting aroma when he returned from work on the pig farm to their first home in a small caravan in the garden of Maggie's parents.

During this time, Peter Wallis and my father visited Tavistock, the town of Arthur's connection with a recently formed 'house church.' However, during the visit Peter decided Tavistock was not the place for Anchor Recordings to move to. On the Saturday afternoon my father was walking around the town and happened on an estate agency. Out of curiosity he went inside, resulting in being handed the particulars of a farm which was up for auction the following week.

That next week my father and David were sat in the auction. They bought a mixed 100 acre Devon farm overlooking the Tamar River into Cornwall, with ideal 'early land' - especially valued for horticulture, as it got the best of the sun in spring and early summer!

Chapter 13

A Farm in far off Devon

This was it! The 'vision' was all of a sudden taking shape: 'Cultural change would make it progressively harder for Christians to survive in our country. Restriction and persecution was well on the horizon.'

God was calling my father and mother to establish an 'Ark' for Christians to prepare for such times. A farm was the perfect setting to learn and provide the basics for life and a new way of living as community It would provide a safe haven in the coming days for persecuted Christians. 'Self sufficiency' was the growing current buzz word.

Lower Birch Farm, however, was significantly run down, due to scant attention over recent years, it was definitely behind the times and somewhat dilapidated, all of which had been reflected in the very attractive price.

Due to his developing chronic heart problems, the previous farmer had reached the point of knowing he had to relinquish what had been in the family for generations, sell and move out. It was little wonder that the farm was in the state that it was.

Completion was to be in two months. Problem. My parents couldn't move from Kent until they had sold their house. My brother, who was buying into the vision was now just starting his one year re-training course in Kent, while his new wife Maggie continued to nurse.

At this time Sue and I, with baby Marc, had now been a couple of months into our new job on a mixed farm in Kent with its' wonderful little modern bungalow on site. It was a marvellous provision for us. I was learning so much and thoroughly enjoying the experience on the fields and with the sheep and cows. Sue and I were settling in and fully expecting to settle there.

Then the suggestion came our way. David said, 'Come and join us in Devon. You can move into the farmhouse and make a start, until the rest of us can join you as able in the next year.'

Sue and I shared our excitement at the prospect of the farm but, in honesty, felt disqualified as we could not go along with the vision. Surprisingly, David and Maggie responded amazingly. 'We ourselves hold the vision lightly and it has to be worked out anyway; it might well be down the line a long way.' Sue and I went away and reflected.

Seriously?

In the middle of December, eight weeks later, we were off again together with all our scant accumulated furniture, our four chickens (in hastily constructed travel accommodation) squeezed into the rented van plus, of course, our treasured eight month old son. The wilds of Dartmoor, winding narrow lanes and steep single tracks, ups and downs through a whole different world, then finally, to the farmhouse.

David and Maggie couldn't join us until David had finished his one year re-training college course in horticulture and agriculture, finishing the next summer. Our parents also couldn't join us either, until they had their house sale.

It was up to Sue and I, wet behind the ears, to make a start managing the land and caring for the small flock of sheep. We had been told lambing was some time in the spring . . . but we didn't know when the ram had been put in with the flock, so we had no idea when lambing might start. Watch and see!

To my shock within four weeks of arrival, something was happening with one of the ewes in the middle of January. Many of the ewes were now well rounded. Speedily, I made some very practical discoveries.

Most of the sheep were Rylands, a relatively rare breed which had been the hobby of the previous owner. Ryland sheep had a very compact conformation, relatively small, but very desirable for the meat trade. Although living locally, due to his ill health I'd never met the previous owner. However, a local man who had worked part-time for him told me, 'He always ran the rams with the ewes all year round. Lambing could happen as and when! But of course some time come spring.'

Something was dawning on me! We had only taken on the flock of sheep, but not the previous farmer's cattle. Following the sale, the whole of the land was the domain of the thirty or so sheep, for the rest of the year. Added to this was, that it was the mildest autumn and winter for years. The grass was lush and plenty of it. The result? The sheep were fat!

Fear not, before leaving the farm in Kent I'd exhausted the farm manager by picking his brains on sheep management and lambing. I now had my copy of the 'TV Vet Book' on sheep; a wonderful hardback of step-by-step photo instructions on everything to do with treating sheep and dealing with lambing, mal-presentations and everything else. Of course, I'd also got the phone number of the nearest vet practice in Tavistock. No problem. Gulp!

The next few months were totally exhausting, exhilarating, heart-breaking, frustrating, humbling and yet fulfilling.

This was well before the days of bringing sheep into barns or sheds as lambing drew near. This was a farm of its era. A small shippon for milking the cows, a couple of open-sided barns for the hay and straw, three 'loose boxes' for large animals and the original stables for the workhorses, made up the farm buildings. The sheep were lambed in the field. If in difficulty, they could be brought into one of the loose boxes for a couple of days until the new lambs were strong enough for the field.

The result: we had every mal-presentation in the book! Farmers want at least doubles or triplets, which is more productive. Rylands are good for producing both. That year was no exception. Added to that, the fact that they were significantly overweight with larger than normal lambs, but having the same opening to venture through into the big wide world and the result was overwhelming. And why was it more often than not at night?

Then there were the foxes. They seemed to love the cheap and easy 'take aways.' Especially when the poor mother had to try and protect three wobbly babies in the dead of night against the expert and wily fox. I speedily got a strong aversion to foxes. Several times during the night, with my pressure lamp in hand, I'd tour the fields making as much noise as I could, counting sheep heads. When I felt especially outraged, I'd add extra visits to fire off my shotgun into the night! I don't think it made the slightest difference - but it made me feel better.

Many long nights were passed seeking to untangle up to twelve different legs inside a speechless mum on the verge of exhaustion. I lost some - truly heart-wrenching. A couple of times in desperation it had to be a visit to the vet the next morning. Amazingly the yield that year was the best we ever had! The mercy of God!

I made a profound discovery about myself over that period. I was a shepherd! It came naturally, it was so invigorating. Up-ending the sheep, steadying them between your legs as you clip their hooves to guard against 'foot rot', 'dagging' their rear ends to keep 'blow-strike' at bay in the summer months. Several times every day visiting them in the fields, watching, checking to see if any were having problems and counting heads. Then, when they were penned in the farmyard, running a hand down their backs, feeling the spines to check their condition and their teeth, to gauge their age and assessing when they were putting on weight enough for market.

Later on, as we were building our new herd of dairy cows, I was discovering something similar to my affinity to the sheep. Handling the cows, getting close and intimate with them - that's what milking is all about. Watching them, observing their behaviour, on their own and also with the herd and, of course, spotting when they are ready for 'service' - the term used for when they were ready for the semen that would be essential for their next calf and then a further nine months of producing milk. Maintaining their health was absolutely of the essence. Regularly at milking time, checking their udder for first signs of the dreaded mastitis became a high priority as we became aware of the danger. Talking to them - mainly politely! Taking care of them. Oh yes, smelling like them too!

It was decades before I began to realise the significance of all this as I was beginning to see that, during those days on the farm, I was functioning in what was innate to me! I was naturally thriving on taking responsibility for these animals and the land that needed to be productive for them. Not only that but it was working!

Sadly, for the longest time, I could not see the personal connection between these experiences and the biblical picture of 'the shepherd of the sheep' that the prophet Ezekiel speaks of in chapter 34. Many centuries later we have the consummate model - Jesus.

Much of my strong aversion to the concept of 'the church pastor', I now realise, was due to the caricature of the real thing I'd seen during those college days in that denominational setting. So many of my fellow students were absolutely not pastors - but they were preparing, with a good heart, to take on the role. It's what was expected of the church leader. It's what we were supposed to do, along with all the preaching, sick visiting, managing the deacons, evangelising and making it all work.

How sad, that it took me so long to face up to what God had made me and what I was!

Chapter 14

Is it Really Dreaming?

A Wonderful Gift: Part of a Body

The Apostle Paul writes to the Corinthian church in his first letter, painting a word picture of the church being like a body. 'For just as the body is one and had many members, and all the members of the body, though many, are one body, so it is with Christ.' (1 Cor. 12:12). He then goes on to apply in practice, the significance of this analogy to the Corinthian Christians, leading up to verse 27, 'Now you are the body of Christ and individually members of it.'

In the next two chapters Paul continues to explain the significance of this multi-gifted body. Everybody has a place to function, for the common good, building up, encouraging and consoling (1 Cor 14:3). No one part of the body is more important than any other part; all are essential for the whole body to be able to function correctly, be healthy and grow. 'If one part suffers, all suffer together; if one member is honoured, all rejoice together.' (1 Cor. 12:26).

This was evidently something that Paul saw as of great significance. Some five or so years later Paul writes to the Ephesian church along similar lines. 'But grace was given to each one of us according to the measure of Christ's gift.' (Eph. 4:7). The context for this earlier in the same

84

chapter underlines how each member of the body is to relate together - in our differences. 'I urge you to walk in a manner worthy of the calling to which you have been called, with all humility and gentleness, with patience, bearing with one another in love, eager to maintain the unity of the Spirit in the bond of peace. There is one body and one Spirit . . .' (Eph 4:1-4).

There are nights when in a half waking state, I dream that maybe, even maybe, God intended his church, his body, to function in this way. I wonder, were the Corinthians and the Ephesians able to hear these exhortations and actually put them into practice and actually relate together in this way? '. . . building up the body of Christ, until we all attain to the unity of the faith and of the knowledge of the Son of God . . .' (Eph 4:13ff)

And Paul doesn't stop there. '. . . Rather, speaking the truth in love, we are to grow up in every way into him who is the head, into Christ . . .' (Eph 4:15 & 16) The head of this amazing dynamic body is Jesus Christ.

I dream. What if, in practice, Jesus really was the 'head' of this body? Not just a titular head, but a head in actual practice and life? What if Jesus was actually directing and facilitating the functioning of every part of this body to fulfil his purposes through his church?

Could it really be that 'church' in practice was made up of every one being the gift that God had created them to be? That the weight did not rest on the few who were teachers or worship leaders? That the 'elders' or ordained ones were no more important than anyone else?

Sorry! I know, I was dreaming. Funny, weird things happen when we are sleeping. But maybe, just maybe, such an experience and practice is for such a time as this.

Chapter 15

Big Challenges!

Come the spring, with their house in Kent sold, my parents joined Sue and I on the farm and we all now squeezed into the farmhouse, plus the dogs. They came with excitement and enthusiasm for the new life. By the end of that summer David and Maggie also joined the gang. After a spell sharing in the farmhouse, they moved into one of the row of old miners' cottages, a few hundred yards away.

Both David and Maggie jumped right in and we bought our first South Devon cow from a farmer the other side of the village. She had calved a month or so before and the farmer kept the calf to rear himself, for beef.

Now we had to start hand milking our first cow. Poor cow! She'd never been hand milked in her life. This was a very strange and unnatural experience for her, added to which, 'where has my dear calf gone?'

The grass was green - and so were we!

We quickly learned how a cow kicks. Not like a horse out the back, but with a nifty rapid 'slam' out of the side, knocking the milker off their little stool and hopefully missing the aluminium churn. We persevered, twice a day. Quickly we learned to adopt the counter intuitive - do not move further away! Get in close, head and arm so close that should she do that rapid leg strike she could hardly move that leg. Lessons were beginning to be learned.

As Bella's milk yield was beginning to build we purchased and installed an in-churn milking machine, attached to a vacuum line in the shippon, and now, providing tempting hay in the feeder, off we went. We were modernising . . . almost.

Something also was going to be learnt very quickly!

We'd bought in a dozen or so more South Devon cows, from a farm some distance away in mid Devon. Two days later after morning milking one of the new cows was in the yard lying on the concrete thrashing her legs and thumping the ground with her head. The poor thing was totally out of control, moaning, in its death throes; we were totally speechless, 'what had we done wrong?'

The vet came quickly. 'She's got red water.' He explained. They were experts in this area, out of necessity. We were in a 'tick-born disease' area. If the calf was born in a 'red water' area the mother would pass on immunity to its calf. They were relatively small areas, mainly in the west Devon area. Cattle born in a 'red water' area would pass the immunity to their progeny. However, animals not born in these areas had no immunity. Almost immediately these cows were brought into these areas, they would be welcomed by the ticks which sucked their blood. The infection would rapidly destroy their red blood corpuscles and within twenty four to thirty six hours the cow would be dead!

This was a really hard, painful and expensive lesson, as it died before our eyes knowing there was nothing we could do to save it; but we learnt quickly!

Whenever a cow was brought onto the farm from outside our immediate area, twice a day at milking time, we would make the cow pass water. If it showed signs of turning red, we 'phoned the vet immediately and he was on site tout suite with the injection to aid it building it's own immunity. It worked every time. The local vets were specialists in 'red water fever,' fortunately.

Soon other lessons became routine for milker and cow. More cows were added, a herd was building. The milk flowed; healthy unpasteurised whole milk straight from the cooler, for all of us. Then the farm ladies mastered making the traditional Devonshire clotted cream. What luxury. Us boys were plenty active, with long physical working days to help keep in check the adverse effects of large quantities of rich whole milk and many fresh baked scones, jam and oodles of clotted cream.

Soon there was far too much whole and skimmed milk for us all to consume. The solution was David's line. He bought in recently weaned piglets from a local farmer. They loved the surplus milk and also scoffed the apples that were flooding in from the acres of old orchard. The time was arriving when we were also producing enough milk to start selling to the Milk Marketing Board, for daily pickups.

The first hay harvest was brought in and connections were continuing to be made with the lively new church in the town, a half a dozen miles away. At that time it was meeting in one of the local homes and was growing rapidly. My father had made contact before we'd moved down and had felt it was definitely fitting with his 'vision' for the farm and it's future.

As we moved into our second year and more cows were being added, David was beginning preparatory work for developing the next project: vegetable and fruit production.

The three of us men were now getting into the routine of meeting in the caravan (now the office) on Monday mornings. This particular Monday morning my father delivered his decision for the way forward.

My Insecurity Hits

As the agricultural side of the farm was developing and David was also progressing with the horticulture, our father was spending much of his time on the developing finance and administration requirements. Dad's qualifications and years of experience were in the higher levels of business and finance. These were his decisions: he would continue to cover the administration and David would take overall charge of the farm. I was surprised. I'd thought that we were in this together, the way we had been doing it for the past months. I was shocked.

The next day I was up in one of the fields repairing a dry stone wall, broken down by the sheep. The painful memory of the day before was deeply imbedded, I'd been demoted; all the feelings of failure and worthlessness from my early years, once more, had been brought to the surface along with the deep pain. I had shared it all with Sue that evening and cooked on it over night. Now, the next day, I could keep it in no longer. With no one in earshot. I howled; I yelled out to God and tears coursed down my desperate face. 'God why have you brought me here? Is this what it's going to be, I'm just the farm worker?' I felt totally broken! I ranted, totally distraught. I tried to verbalise to God my deep, confused feelings of disappointment and hopelessness. Here they were again, those repeated memories surfacing of feeling inadequate, not coming up to the mark, a failure - hearing those deep sighs from a father, whom I'd let down again! Deep painful memories of that day, three times every year, when the school report landed on the mat.

All I could do was try to cover it up. Work as usual. However, something must have seeped out. A few days later my brother David had a chat with me. I'd calmed down a bit, but had tried to communicate my surprise at the turn of events.

At the next Monday meeting, David took my side, suggesting that he major on developing the horticulture and market garden side and I major on the cows and the land management - but we were all to be in it together. Masterful and so gracious. Indeed, the years ahead proved that we needed each other. However, my deep insecurity had been side-stepped, but not fixed.

In due course it came up at a Monday morning meeting; father clarified: we were to continue as we were - David heading up the horticulture and me the cows and managing the land.

What had all that been about? It all seemed to have been so unnecessary. However, the reality of it was, I was being confronted by my deep-seated vulnerabilities. It was years later that my ever so gracious heavenly Father was highlighting all these areas in a context I could face and find healing and progressive wholeness for who I was. Does God work 'in all situations' for the very best for us His children? Absolutely Yes. But I did not realise it at the time. 'Me, damaged goods, like everyone else on this planet? No way!'

Chapter 16

Life and Death - Six Years Flash By

The next four years was a time of amazing development, change and hard work.

The South Devon cows went, replaced by a larger herd of Friesian and Holstein milking cows. We laid hundreds of square metres of concrete farmyard by hand, the large silage clamp for all the winter feed requirements and installed the new milking parlour and a bulk milk tank to hold and refrigerate the days yield. Fortunately, contractors erected the 'cow kennels,' housing for the new herd. Oh yes, the hand milking was definitely a thing of the past!

The full time team of workers grew. There were three of us managing the cows and farm area, two running the horticulture venture and two managing the farm shop in the nearby town.

More acres were added and we became more proficient, so the cows became more productive.

Dad was fully occupied with the accounts and all the business details.

The horticulture was the most surprising development. The different polythene tunnels were growing early strawberries, tomatoes, courgettes, lettuce, peppers and other vegetables. There were also various soft fruits and rhubarb along with the several acres of main crop strawberries.

It was David's task to drive the produce to the vegetable and fruit market in Plymouth come evening time. There was also supplying the farm produce to the new fruit and veg shop David and Maggie had set up in nearby Tavistock. Fortunately Dad stocked the stall at the farm gate, plus various other items - apples in the season and jams produced in the farmhouse or sold to friends, and, of course, the home baked cakes - sadly they didn't last long before they went - there were never any left over at the end of the day for us!

Things had developed well with the now significant sized church in the nearby town, with all the farm families also being involved in the church. Another couple from the church had taken on the management of the fruit & veg shop. Sue and I were now invited to lead one of the small groups in the growing church. At that time, small groups were a very radical new departure. It was a whole new ball game. What made it more difficult was the number; twenty people sat around the large front room, not knowing quite what to expect! It was a profound new learning experience.

A year or so later came a massive 'rocker.' David felt he could no longer carry on with the horticulture. The constant repetitive field work and hard physical slog, had been taking its toll. He felt forced to face the implications of all this, successful though it was, for the rest of his life. It was not him! David was a people person. He'd excelled in school teaching, before a whim of adventure lured him as an officer into the army, only to be consigned to junior soldiers

- this was certainly no place for an enthusiastic historian. Despite everything, both David and Maggie were convinced he should go back to school teaching.

Eventually, they both left for a one term post in an excellent school in Bath. Rod had been working with David for the previous few years. With his college training in horticulture, Rod was more than willing to take over managing on the farm. This made complete sense, Rod was fulfilling what he'd been trained for.

Seismic Shock

The very next year there was a strong disagreement between the main church leader and my father. It culminated with a hastily convened meeting one Saturday morning when the whole church was called together. With a visiting apostle supporting, the main leader announced that my father and mother were being 'put out of the church.' They were to be 'shunned'; they were not allowed to attend any meetings and no one was to have anything to do with them, at all, in any setting! I for my part was completely staggered and shocked; I just could not believe it! Ok, dad was always very black and white with his views, but this was totally absurd.

The farm was divided. Some felt they should stay with the church, hence they were not permitted to have anything to do with my father. Sadly, Rod who had been driving the horticulture along with his wife, felt they could not continue working on the farm and still be a part of the church in these circumstances, so they promptly left. At least a third of the church also left in utter shock.

We had to adjust on the farm immediately. There was no one to continue the horticulture; there was only one

93

choice, I had to step up and take over. Learn and do it. The other two guys who had been working with me in the dairy didn't want to continue with the church and were settled on the farm. They willingly continued what they had already learnt, managing the dairy cows and followers over past months.

I, for my part, had so much to learn, quickly. There was always a lot to water, harvest and market. Spring had passed and we were doing well going into the next summer.

Several months later, one day in late May, I was working in one of the polythene tunnels and the inevitable took over. I flipped. I knew it - I couldn't continue. The pressures were far too great. The heart breaking demise within the church; the broken relationships and shattered dreams of what God was doing, along with the immense work pressures, had been taking their toll on me. I lay on the ground in that polythene tunnel, amongst the tomato plants and was bawling my heart out. Father appeared, having heard the noise. As the emotion and painful tears poured out all I could bawl was 'I can't carry on. I can't carry on. It's all too much for me. I can't carry on'. His reaction was surprisingly swift; after just a few minutes of listening to my conclusion, with pained face he responded: 'We'll sell up then'.

Early in September the farm went to auction. There was a good attendance. The three of us, father, David and I sat and observed from the back of the auction room. The auctioneer did a great job; he had obviously spotted the really serious bidder. Of course, this was a Devon farming community and the one he had spotted would have been well known to him. He would have known that this farmer had already sold his farm and was looking for a new location. A point came in the bidding when he pulled a few bids out of the air to enhance the price. Of course, it was out of our hands and it sold for a very good price. In six years the price of land had risen very significantly. It was so encouraging that, after all we had invested in effort, sweat and money it had paid off in such a strange way.

At the end of October we had the farm sale. All the cows and followers, along with all the farm machinery was up for sale. The cows were autumn calvers and many had just calved and were coming into their best yielding months with many others very close to calving. They were all at their peak of desirability, their value enhanced with the daily records of all their previous milk yields. The sale went amazingly well and surpassed all our expectations. It was all amazing; but so sad and definitely emotional. In two days we would leave.

Wonderfully, my brother along with Maggie, had just started a permanent teaching post. An amazing God opening; teaching history and also in charge of the combined cadet force in a top English school. It was so good they were there with us to witness the final days on the farm. For me, much was a blur. How strange it had been walking the cows, one at a time, around the sale ring, hearing rising prices on these numbered animals. They were not just numbers; I knew each of them intimately; they had names, characters and memories were evoked, some good, some painful and, 'Gosh, 'I'm not going to be smelling like this at the end of each day!'

'Heavenly Father, here we are once again; what have you got now for Sue and I plus, our now two, young boys? What a crazy journey we are on! So many total direction changes in our lives. 'God are you really in all this, or is it all just our stupidity?'

Chapter 17

Doubt!

Can any Good Come ?

Does God really work all things together for good?

Categorically, I can absolutely reply with a great big 'Yes!' I stand shoulder to shoulder with Paul! 'We know that for those who love God all things work together for good, for those who are called according to his purpose.' (Rom 8:28)

But, not to mislead you, such confidence has not always been my position and even this has not been easily won. There have been many times, as I look back, when I have seriously doubted the intent and even ability of my heavenly Father, to bring good out of chaos and despair. Maybe, like me, you have an Honours Degree in 'Doubt!'

Here's the big one. Doubt is not all bad. These two go together - 'doubt' and 'faith'. You can't have faith without the reality and prospect of doubt. To put it another way, 'Is doubt sin?' Doubt is a consequence of our fallen humanity, what Paul the Apostle refers to as our 'flesh'. We can choose to live according to our flesh, or rely on God's amazing provision, through Jesus, the Holy Spirit - his power in us as Christians. Easy? No way! It seems that the whole journey of life is opportunity to learn this lesson, in practice, more and more.

Doubt is like a springboard in a great big swimming pool. There's a shallow end and a deep end. You're not the best of swimmers but you are getting better at it; not just in the shallow end, but more and more feeling confident as you master the goal of venturing from the shallow to the deep end, turning and then making it back into your depth.

Over the next week you are stirred with the idea of those diving boards and the way that even kids climb the ladders and jump, with a scream of delight, as they plunge into the deep below. 'Yes, I'm going to try that next time. It looks so much fun!'

The next visit to the pool arrives. Eventually you walk down the pool side toward the deep end, with your heart beating ninety-nine to the dozen, looking at that springboard - 'no, that's not too high above the water.' Tentatively you edge towards the end of the board, looking apprehensively into the water beneath; it's well out of your depth. Worse still, as you reach the end of the board it's wobbling more and more under your feet. You feel very unstable, so vulnerable and common sense is making its powerful case - 'back off; you can swim anyway; you don't need to do this!' This is 'doubt' in action!

From the security of the solid ground you watch what others are doing. They don't walk tentatively. They run the length of the board, bounce on the end and fly high into the air and enter the water - most of them feet first.

'I'm going to do it, I'm going to do it.' You mount the board, run at it, bounce on the end, soar into the air and plunge into the deep water. This is 'trust' in the face of 'doubt'. As you sink below the water your whole body experiences a wonderful feeling of elation, silence and awe, as the water gently eases you back to the surface. You grab some air and think, 'Wow, I'm going to do that again.'

These two go together. Doubt can be so good - the springboard into the experience of demanding trust, resulting in faith in action; 'No, the board will not break just as I jump and the water will not harm me; I will come back up to the surface in time to breath again!' As disciples of Jesus, our trust, our faith is not in a springboard, in an object, a philosophy, right teaching or wishful thinking - it's in a person. It's the very One through whom we were created for this actual thing - a personal relationship of trust with him and his Father. It's through the 'springboards' of life that we prove and grow in the experience, knowledge and confident certainty that our great God can and will bring good out of every situation, even the hard and the very bad ones.

Oh, yes, 'In all things God does work together for good for those who love him and are called according to his purposes.'

Chapter 18

The Plan Continues to Unfold

Penryn and Sunrise

We left the farm, Sue and I with our two boys, Marc and Tim, and set off westwards across the River Tamar, over which we had gazed for those years from the top fields of the farm into Cornwall.

So much happened over the next ten years; so much contrast; so many more experiences and different places; heart-breaking disappointments and sadnesses, but also amazing divine provision and interventions. How our heavenly Father enables good and wonderful surprises out of failures and disillusions. So much evidence that God does indeed 'work in all things together for good for those who love him and are called according to his purposes.'

Sue's parents, were now attending the Baptist Church in Falmouth, Cornwall, having recently moved down from west London. They passed on to us that they had heard there was a small 'House Church' meeting in Penryn and they thought it might suit us. We checked it out on a visit while looking for a house. At that time there were about six couples with various aged children and one single lady. They met together on a Sunday morning in a home. There was singing and looking at the Bible, followed by lunch altogether and then a walk in the afternoon among the wonderful scenery that's Cornwall. It was great - building friendships with Jesus at the centre. It was a no-brainer. So refreshing after all the pain and sadness we had come from.

Wonderfully, we were able to buy a house with a mortgage in Penryn, which we moved into on leaving the farm. A suggestion from one of the new Group we had joined, resulted in Sue and I taking over a shop unit in the nearby City of Truro. Who would have guessed that? It had been going for just a year and, sadly, the couple who had started it selling Third World craft goods were divorcing and had to give the shop up. My parents put some money into the small business and the outstanding lease, with some of the proceeds of the farm sale. We went into partnership together with dad doing the books. They had moved from Devon to Wiltshire. I was sending dad the weekly sales and outgoings by post and the arrangement was working perfectly.

We started by making changes to the shop layout, with a third of the floor area given over to Christian books and music, which fitted with one of my passions. The rest of the space was filled with the many hand crafted items from Bangladesh, India and other countries supported by Tear Fund and Tear Craft. Off we went. It was the start of another amazing stage in our journey. Sue and I were in no doubt at all, that God's hand was on all this. We could never have guessed how everything was fitting together.

Within three years we'd moved location to a prime site in the city. The Third World crafts had come to a natural end quite quickly, as the market and interest changed. We took on greeting cards and a wide range of gift items including the growing trends of the time: stickers and stationary items which were all the rage for kids. We did wonderfully well, and the cream on the cake was being able to give more space for the christian books, cassettes and then CDs. We were now employing five full time staff and a part time book keeper.

Sadly, after two years with the House Church a conflict arose between the two men who had started it and it soon became evident that there was no future for us there.

During this period there were monthly 'Renewal Meetings' on a Saturday evening in a Truro Parish Church. The meetings were well supported from the whole of central and western Cornwall by people from across the denominational divide. A nationally well known speaker visited each time from the diverse charismatic movement that was gathering momentum during the 1980's. They were such encouraging times. Praise, led by a local band, set the scene for memorable Friday and Saturday evenings with David Pawson, Don Double, Colin Urquhart and many other speakers. A particularly memorable weekend was with David Watson in Truro Cathedral.

There was one occasion when an American, with his wife, who were staying for a few weeks in the city with a local family, spoke on the Friday evening and also at the Saturday renewal meeting, as was normal, but also there were two extra sessions on Saturday morning and afternoon, at a local centre. I was so encouraged by the Friday evening session that I decided to attend the morning and afternoon sessions on the Saturday as well. I was captivated by what he was sharing from Ezekiel Chapter 34, about the practice of the shepherd and his sheep, relating the passage to Jesus as the chief shepherd and then applying it to the Church today. He was ringing all my bells. Yes, this is what it is to be a shepherd in the biblical sense.

It turned out that the speaker, Mark McGrath and his wife Chris, were staying with a family who felt that God was leading them to start a new church, reaching the City of Truro. Sue and I found out more. The timing was perfect. We said our goodbyes to the folks in Penryn that September and joined this small group of about a dozen folk in Truro, who were now just starting to meet up in a home.

A year or so later an interesting event happened.

Chapter 19

Our God of Surprises and Impeccable Timing

One drizzly Monday morning, during our second year in the shop, I opened up as usual, set the stands up outside in the shopping centre walkway and set to with the dusting as normal. Almost immediately a young man appeared in the wide front entrance, with suitcase in hand and headed for me. As always I moved behind the counter. He put his suitcase down on the other side of the counter, introduced himself and began to tell me his story. My visitor said he had just escaped and fled from the 'Moonies,' a cult that was prevalent at that time. He said he had to get as far away as possible, hence Cornwall.

He recounted how bad it had turned out to be, after several years of 'brainwashing.' He'd come to 'Sunrise' because it was a Christian shop. The day passed as usual but in between serving customers, he filled me in with all the details of his past few years and how he wanted to get 'Jesus: the real thing.' It just so happened that the flat in the basement of our house had recently become vacant, due to the young couple living there moving on. I called Sue, explained the situation and we agreed we could offer Joseph a bed for the night. He accepted the offer with enthusiasm.

Joseph turned out to be very personable and fitted in well with the family - Sue and I, plus our two young sons.

The next morning he came with me to the shop and within a day or two, was even serving customers with me. Wednesday evening came when Mark McGrath, who we were getting to know, was visiting Truro from the States and was teaching that evening in the new Truro church. Very kindly Joseph offered to babysit the boys so Sue and I, along with the young lady who was also lodging with us at that time, could all go to the meeting. Come Friday it was really helpful to have support in the shop, so I could pop over to the bank to pay in the takings.

Saturday was as busy as ever but I was coping, so Joseph went out for his break. There were no customers in the shop just at that time and it was doubly great to see our friend Mark appear at the entrance - it would be so good to catch up with him. However I was surprised that it was not the normal friendly Mark. 'Where's Joseph, Barry?' Surprised, I replied, 'He's gone out for a break.' 'That's good' was his response. 'A police detective sergeant is coming in to see you.' 'What! What's happened?' I said. 'He'll fill you in, but Joseph is not quite what he makes himself out to be,' was Mark's response as he apologetically took his leave. About half an hour later the policeman arrived and told me that Joseph had been arrested!

Shock is a mild term to describe what I felt. He informed me that Joseph had been apprehended and was being interviewed, under caution, at the local police station. That was all he could tell me at that time; he added that Sue had allowed the police to search our home and there was no need to worry. Then he left.

An hour or so later, as if I wasn't shocked enough and grappling with a spinning head, Terry a friend of ours appeared in the doorway and come in with a broad grin.

'Terry what are you doing here - you're a long way from Yorkshire?' I said. Terry had become a good friend while he was posted to the Royal Airforce base close to Truro and then had been moved to Yorkshire. He'd married a lovely Norwegian lady and they were settled in that area. Terry proceeded to tell me the story. Mercifully, at that time in the afternoon, the shop had gone quite quiet.

Apparently some nine months earlier Joseph had appeared at the church which Terry and his wife Katy attended. Terry, being a personable and caring person, on hearing his story of woe, had taken Joseph into their three story terraced Victorian home where there was a basement room ideal for him.

As the weeks passed their lodger made a profession of faith in Jesus and was baptised. The Bevan family treated him as part of their family. Just a week ago, while Joseph had been out, they had cause to go into his room looking for something they thought they had left in his cupboard. To their utter shock they found in the back of the cupboard, hidden behind Joseph's clothes, a stash of the family's belongings: Jewellery, food, treasured possessions, a hundred and one items which amazingly had not been missed. On seeing it all, they realised, there had been times when they couldn't find things they were looking for, but never dreamt Joseph could have been the reason. That evening when their children had gone to bed, after Joseph had gone to his room, Terry went down to confront him. He wasn't there. His suitcases, clothes and everything else had all gone. He'd realised he'd been rumbled.

A couple of days later, Terry drove down to Cornwall to stay in the bungalow he still owned, which had been his home during his posting in the area. The next morning he walked into our shop and spotted Joseph behind the counter talking to me. Unnoticed by either of us, he beat a hasty retreat and notified the local police, telling them the story. The police had then contacted Sue and searched our flat where Joseph had been staying. They found many of the possessions Terry had described, secreted away under the ceiling space, below the floor of our living room above; along with some of our belongings. Our lodger, on checking in her chest of drawers, confirmed that certain things had been moved and rearranged, but thought nothing had been taken.

Later in the afternoon the policeman called to inform me that Joseph had received several charges, including theft, and was being detained until a court appearance. In due course he was given a twelve month prison sentence. This had not been his first run in with the Law.

We never saw Joseph again after that Saturday, but we were so reassured and encouraged! What a wonderful heavenly Father we have. Maybe we were foolish in taking Joseph in and trusting him. Maybe it would have been wiser to check him out and not respond in welcoming him into our home and leaving him in the shop on his own. A shiver still goes down my spine as I think of that Wednesday evening when we left our two young boys in his care - with opportunity to go through our bedrooms too, as he certainly had done so in our lodgers' room as she had confirmed that some things were not as she had left them.

Despite all, our heavenly Father was watching over us. It is absolutely amazing, that Terry would be 'inspired' to drive the seven hour, three hundred mile journey all the way to Cornwall, carrying a sense that Joseph was there and I was the first person he contacted!

What a lesson in experiencing God's protection and care, even in the little details. It transpired that the shop was over a hundred pounds short and several pounds of book tokens were missing. I would have put it down to experience, but my dad contacted the insurers and, following an interview, they made up the complete value of the loss, even though, with a grin, the agent said that he was stretching it a bit for us!

What a lesson. Even despite our naivety or even stupidity, it was definitely preparation for so many more situations still to come of testing and trusting, in a Father like none other.

Chapter 20

Miraculous Provision

By the next spring it was absolutely clear that we should move to Truro. This was definitely now the focus of our lives. The shop was going well and the small church was beginning to grow. Meeting in the home was now impractical for the numbers getting involved, the evident need was to find some rented space to meet in. House prices were now beginning to rise; Truro prices were certainly higher than where we were currently living. 'Father, what have you got for us? Do you want us to move to Truro? Is it what you've really got for us?'

Liz, a young lady, was now working in the shop part time. In passing, I mentioned our intentions to move to Truro. The next time she came in to work she shocked me! 'I mentioned it to my dad,' she said, 'and he and my mum agree, they want you to have their house in Truro; they need to move to another town where my dad's got a new job.' I asked where in Truro their house was. 'It's in The Avenue and quite close to the city centre.' I laughed out loud - very rude of me; I knew where The Avenue was, a private road with large Victorian houses, and very nice too. What could I say? 'How much are they wanting for it?' 'I'll ask them' she replied.

The next day Liz came in to work and announced 'They do want you to have it and are asking for

£30,000.' 'No way Liz,' I replied 'it must be worth far more than that!' That evening I told Sue. The only reason we had been able to get the house we were currently in, was because of the share of the farm proceeds my parents had given my brother, my sister and me.

Due to having no savings and no credit history, it would have been impossible for Sue and I to have qualified for any sort of mortgage when we had moved from the farm. With our £10,000 share we had a great down payment, but no way was that enough, alongside my very modest wage from the shop. Graciously my parents had also offered a £9,000 loan for the balance so that we could buy our first house in Penryn, those three years before. Now adding these two figures together we were still a long way short of the £30,000! Sue and I agreed that, maybe we ought to go and see the house, so we made an appointment to view it. It turned out to be a semi-detached end of row property built in 1880 with three stories and a basement, four bedrooms, a significant back garden with grand conker trees, grassed area (great for cricket and games for the kids) and a dilapidated garage at the side. Oh yes, a large felled tree still lay across the grassed area with broken glass everywhere from the recently renewed first floor veranda roof!

The inside was definitely 'tired', needing plenty of redecoration. But what a space. What potential. Large rooms ideal for everything! 'Heavenly Father what is this about? Could you just be in this?'

The next day we thought we'd give it a try. Nothing would be lost. I went to a Building Society in the city, at random, filled in an application form and walked out, bemused. A few days later the 'phone rang 'Mr Heaton, in relation to the property on your mortgage application form, we've had it valued and . . . did you know, the current market value is 35% higher than the asking price?' I replied that I actually didn't. His response was matter of fact. They would supply the £10,000 mortgage and set the wheels in motion!

A few months later with our Penryn house sold and all the paperwork sorted, we moved into The Avenue, Truro. An excellent Primary School was a short walk up the road and the walk down the hill to our shop was just ten minutes away. What a marvellous God provision it truly was!

Chapter 21

Christian Community Church Truro

The new church grew rapidly. Folk were coming from a widening area outside of the city. There was a definite buzz of new life and vitality. The new songs, coming into churches in the early and mid-eighties, were welcomed with enthusiasm. Within a year, the home meeting on a Sunday was past bursting point; soon the recently rented space in an office was out-grown too, with fear that the volume of people and the bouncing of the floor in worship, would result in an unwelcome fall into the basement any moment! After six months there, we rented Sunday space in a local Sports Hall. Growth just continued.

Time passed and still growing, I felt honoured to join the existing leader to make up a two-man eldership. Many highly gifted people joined us; the number of small groups expanded and our Sunday attendees were well into the second hundred. A growing number of people were joining us from the towns around Truro.

Mark and his wife, Chris, continued to encourage us with regular visits from the States and many from the church also made visits to the States in return, to see what they were doing in their city, Newburgh on the Hudson River, in upper New York State. When Sue and I, plus our now three kids, went for a three week stay, the church folk there went out of their way to make us feel very welcome. It was great. The grand finale on our last day was definitely memorable because of the very different food our hosts gave us, before we flew back to the UK that night. Being Thanksgiving Day we had pumpkin pie on top of oodles of turkey and all the trimmings! Just as we were saying our goodbyes to our hosts, one of our boys was violently sick in the lounge, to our great embarrassment. For the flight back to the UK, each of our stomachs was making its presence well felt - ugh!

Back in Truro, one of the highlights of our life at that time, for Sue and I was the relationships established with the small group, we were both leading. So many of these relationships have continued over the decades since. It wasn't just the Thursday evening meetings, we did things together, along with the abundance of kids as well. Especially memorable was the wonderful long weekend away we all spent together at a holiday retreat centre further down the coast. Week by week, real issues in people's lives were being faced, in the meetings, but especially in time spent together over food; or whatever the ladies got up to during the day. Sue was so good at relating to people. It was a very special time. Dutifully, after every meeting, I wrote the required report on what had happened at the meeting and submitted it to the main leader.

In due time another elder was established. Now there were three of us. Sadly, the dynamics within the new leadership team remained as it had been. Up to this time I'd thought that maybe the way things functioned between us as elders was because of me - and I was reluctant to make an issue of what I was feeling and seeing of equality within eldership.

Our new colleague was not as reticent as I was. After a few months, I found myself having to act as the buffer between my two colleagues. The main man had to be the main man! He expected the two of us to toe his line and just fit in. I sought as much as I could not to be divisive, but began to realise how inappropriately I had behaved over the previous years, when there was just the two of us. It dawned on me that I had been carefully sowing ideas and suggestions and watering them, where necessary, in such a way that, if something materialised in that direction in due course, it would be his idea. With this growing realisation I was horrified at my behaviour. I'd been manipulating. Now I was in a dilemma. I had been using just another form of control! Born of frustration and desire to do good and be true to myself - but none the less grievous to my heavenly Father.

Facing Up

That day is indelibly printed in my memory; we'd shut up the shop and I was walking home with Mark who was to join us for tea before the evening meeting. He was over from the States, for one of his frequent visits to encourage the church with teaching, wise words and insights.

We'd just crossed the busy road and were about to walk up the steep hill that led to our house. I was feeling super nervous, anxious of telling Mark how I was really feeling and also knowing I'd been mega guarded with Mark as well; I finally knew I had to risk it.

I started, and it all came out - I told him how I felt it was in the eldership; how it was in the church and my feelings of being useless and repressed by the well-meaning leader. I carefully did not use the word 'control', maybe I should have, but I didn't need to. Just before we reached our house, no questions asked, Mark stated 'You must all come over and spend time with us at Newburgh.' I was stunned. Later when Sue and I were together and the kids had gone to bed, he clarified what he was offering 'Come for a year - be a part of the church. In the meantime come over for a month or so and check us out a bit more and prepare for the longer spell.'

As soon as possible we went for that month. We stayed with Mark, his wife, three children and extended family. They were so hospitable and put themselves out for us; as a family we felt we just fitted in. The church there had grown significantly since our first visit and had recently moved into a large old city library building that the church folks were now renovating. If there had been any doubts before about making the 'Big Move,' when we got back to UK all doubts were gone.

There were, however, many obstacles that had to be overcome - but it was a no brainer! Sue and I were together in it with faith and excitement. If it was a God-thing it would all fit together.

Challenges and Confirmation

One by one we faced the practicalities of the big move. Sadly, my parents, who were partners in the shop business, strongly stated that they could not agree to us going to the States - 'spiritually' it would be walking into 'the lions den.' Sue and I felt we could not submit to their opinion; there was only one way forward - we would have buy them out.They were shocked and horrified that we didn't fall in line with their perspective. We set them free.

To rent our house to a tenant demanded that we updated our Victorian, three storey basement property. At the least it needed more re-decorating. The hall and massive three storey landing were dismal and dark. No way did we have the the money to pay for contractors. Amazingly, Mark arranged for a half-dozen of the men from the Newburgh church to come over for a week and help us out at their expense. Accommodation was volunteered by members of our church. They did a wonderful job - all three floors of hall, stairs and landings were transformed. A whole new breath of life now affected the whole house. That week also cemented relationships that had already started with these guys. Later, Sue and I decorated some of the other rooms that were in dire need.

Pete, who'd been with me in the shop almost from the start, agreed to take on it's management, leading the staff of five full-time and part-time workers. He'd done a great job with the rest of the team while we'd been away and had definitely come into his own. Wonderfully, every detail came together, including a young couple in the church agreeing to rent our house while we were away for that year.

July came and we flew off to another world! Graciously, the Truro church leader and the other elder released us and agreed to give us some financial support while we were gone for the year, on the understanding that I would remain an elder in absentia and they would keep me in the loop as to how the church was going while we were away.

Gradual Dawning
I was beginning to realise something that had been a common and natural part of my life. However, I was not

sure and certainly not clear as to whether it was right or wrong. I was being confronted with something from the world that I was in; but also recognising that it was a part of me.

As the years passed I was seeing more and more that this was one of the 'Big Cs'.

Chapter 22

Newburgh, New York State

A lovely older couple from the church picked us up from JFK Airport, in their large sedan and drove us north to Mark and Chris's home. They squeezed us into their now even more extended family; our boys were to sleep in the attic and our daughter, Hannah, to share a room with little Jenny, who was the same age. Sue and I were much blessed at having a bedroom all to ourselves, plus the inevitable electric fan which was necessary to be able to sleep at all.

We were made to feel so at home and we really felt it. The three lodgers, also part of the household, were single ladies, all with different jobs in the area; added to this Mark and Chris with their three children and now Sue and I plus three more kids - this was quite a special family! My day started early, along with Mark, in the church office with various meetings. My first surprise was to be welcomed in the early morning elders meeting as a fellow elder to the current team of three.

The high spot of the family was the evening meal together around the very large dining table, often with other church folk joining to eat. The great family meal was finally followed with time for the household to gather and relax at 10pm and watch the new and much loved Jay Letterman Late Show, for the next hour.

It was a big surprise when within two weeks, one of the other three elders resigned due to the developments in his job which were taking him more and more all over the country. That left Mark, Pete and now me. Something else was becoming evident, especially in the evenings; Mark was spending long periods of time listening and talking with different people on the 'phone. The 'phone was in the open living space so we couldn't but help hearing Mark's counsel for various people from one of the family of churches in another State. It seemed that different folk in this church were struggling to cope with real difficulties just at that time. This was one of the largest group of churches in New Jersey and was also a part of Edification Ministries; it was exploding. This particular church was made up of churches in Vermont, north towards the Canadian border, a plant in London as well as the main church in New Jersey.

Financial irregularities were coming to light. The main leader had now resigned and many of the elders were being disgraced for their part in syphoning off monies from the lucrative cleaning business that members of the church had been 'encouraged' to work for. This group of large churches was in a process of disintegration and the many hundreds of church members were totally distraught. Mark was personable and approachable and so many folks were turning to him for his caring ear and counsel. The whole area of trust and the authority of leaders and elders was now in question. Most members scattered in the weeks that followed and many walked away from Jesus as a result. Heartbreaking. Appropriate questions were being posed.

Chapter 23

A Wild Night

One Friday that summer, Dolores, the church secretary answered the 'phone in the church office. It was an English man visiting New York who wanted to attend the church, could he speak to someone? Mark was on holiday with the family so Dolores put the call through to me.

The man's name was Raoul, he'd recently become a Christian in the UK, was a musician and was touring the US with Elton John; he said he would like to visit our church on Sunday. Raoul went on to say that it had been a long concert programme, touring from the west coast to the east coast of the States and he was exhausted. The final concert, in Maddison Square Gardens, New York City, was on the coming Sunday night. He'd had no fellowship with christians - far from it, and he was now struggling big time. Sue and I had been leant the use of a car for a few weeks, so I suggested the two of us should drop in to see him the next day, Saturday; it was only a 70 mile drive south. He jumped at the suggestion and gave us the address of the hotel he was staying in and we agreed a time to meet there the next day.

Raoul was so open and honest with us and said he was feeling very vulnerable and depressed. He lived in Sussex, England, and was a professional trumpeter. On returning from a previous concert tour of the Far East with Wham, Raoul had 'an episode' during the jet flight which had caused no end of problems and hit the headlines. On his return to the UK he had connected with some Christians and subsequently given his life to Jesus and was now attending the New Frontiers Church in Brighton with his wife. He was fearful that the couple of months in the touring context was having too heavy a toll on him.

Sue and I listened to the wonderful details of how God had so evidently broken into Raoul's life and that of his wife, who was a classical musician. We prayed with him and sought to encourage him as much as we could. We assured him of a warm welcome with us the next day, if he could find a way of getting the 70 miles north, up to Newburgh. He eagerly said he would rent a car and be with us. True to his word, Raoul arrived at the church building on time and joined with us for the meeting the next morning. Evidently the meeting was similar to what he was now used to in Sussex. It was good to see him so positive and light as we concluded the meeting - very different from the day before. We went out for lunch afterwards. He couldn't stay long as he had to be at the venue mid afternoon to prepare for the evening performance. Before leaving he invited Sue and I to be his guests that evening, at the final Elton John concert of the US Tour. Wow.

'Are you sure Raoul? We haven't got tickets?' we asked. 'No problem; you'll be my special guests,' was his reply.

That morning after the meeting, Raoul had invited another couple to come to the concert as well. That afternoon the four of us set off for the drive south with Raoul's parting words: 'Meet me at 7.00 this evening, at the rear stage door and I'll get you the special guest passes.' True to his word Raoul appeared from inside, explained to the guard on the stage door that we were his guests and then told us to follow him through a labyrinth of passageways and up a few floors. Raoul then handed us each a posh looking card with 'Special Guest' printed in large letters. We hung these around our necks and pushed through growing throngs of people back stage with all sorts of titles of their official job descriptions dangling from their necks. Finally we made our entrance through the back of the stage, to the enormous, famous, Maddison Square Gardens.

It was breathtaking. The stage was massive with a raised central part at the back and a large horseshoe apron area spreading into a sizeable empty space, then the front rows of seats backed with many banks of seats rising to the roof. Laid out on the raised central area was a row of microphones on stands, with more rows of mics on stands, along with instrument stands for a range of instruments on the left of the apron. In front of everything, stood the large grand piano.

The plan had been for seats for the four of us. However, this was the final tour date, the Big One! The stage manager said that as all the seats were booked, we would have to stand where we were, but move out of the way of people coming in and out from back stage. We didn't have front seats - we were right on the massive stage!

There was still some time to go before the start. 'Oh there's Mick Jagger and, yes, there's so and so'. The great and the good were mingling. Looking at our 'Guest' cards we saw that we were also included in the After Event Party. What was that going to look like?

Eventually there was action, with the appropriate cheers and clapping as the backing singers took their places behind the mics on the central raised area next to the

122

drummer; the musicians took up their places behind the piano, with more cheers - and, yes, there was Raoul warming up his trumpet alongside the other wind instruments and various guitarists.

The massive twenty thousand plus audience began to settle and then came the big entrance: Elton, in his Elton attire, danced onto centre stage, bowing, raising his hands and yelling something, but no way making the slightest dent into the deafening, cheering, yelling and clapping of the audience now to a person on its feet.

Finally, the crowd began to quieten as Elton dramatically got himself comfortable behind the grand and he was off. The overall effect was electrifying. All the old and the more recent Elton classics; the spine-chilling sound of the backing singers, the band plus Elton's distinctive voice and piano playing, all went to create the amazing experience. Being a matter of feet away from the action, and then to turn at right angles and see the massive audience, layer upon layer, up to the far distant roof was awesome. The band was certainly not too shabby either; they had their moments when the focus was on their different instruments taking the lead. The big difference came when it was Raoul's turn; not just the wonderful expressive sound, but the action - as he danced into the centre of the stage with trumpet in the air waving it around as he played. Of course, the audience loved it and just added to the screams and cheers as the song continued and Elton came back in with the words and thumping chords.

The hours passed and then came the grand finale to round it all off. Our two friends and Sue and I were in total agreement as it came to an end. Although we were all exhausted, standing for all those hours, the songs, the emotion of it all, the spectacle we had witnessed and feeling such a part of it was wonderful. Well worth every minute.

Now what? Eventually Raoul appeared and announced that there was the big end of tour celebration party upstairs, but he didn't want to go to it. 'Lets go and get something to eat' he said. The time didn't seem to be relevant, it was now well past midnight and yes we were hungry. We all piled into our car and Raoul directed us to Greenwich Village; he wanted to go to a Japanese restaurant. A Japanese restaurant it was - he knew exactly where to go.

'Will it be open still, the area seems quite deserted?' I asked.

'No problem' he replied. 'Pull in by the side of the road, you can park here, the restaurant is just a couple of doors down.' As we all got out I looked about, I expressed my concern about parking in this no parking street.

'No problem,' he replied 'this is Greenwich Village and it's after midnight'.

We went into the restaurant for, yet, another first for Sue and I - Japanese food: what is this going to be like? We were well up for something else new and it was very special. Evidently not a first for Raoul, he knew what to order and explained how we were to eat it - we enthusiastically joined the journey. Another great, unforgettable experience.

It was coming up to 3.00am when we got back to the car, to take Raoul back to his hotel. What a truly memorable evening it had been. The parking ticket on the windscreen just adding to it. Raoul took it from me, tore it up and threw it into the gutter saying it didn't count. He got that bit wrong though!

It was quite a few years later when, talking to a friend from a church in Brighton, that the name Raoul was mentioned; both Raoul and his wife were still going on with Jesus. How good to hear.

Chapter 24

Could We Trust Him? Big Time!

Evangelism Training Program

Into the month of September the first ETP Program started in the Newburgh church. The Evangelism Training Program, Mark's initiative, was running for the next year and had drawn together twenty year olds from across the churches, including one from the UK. I was given the pastoral responsibility for the team.

It was a great year. Teaching, mainly from Mark, with a reading programme, morning classes and afternoon practical activities, along with a few weeks of 'doing it' in the UK and periods of time away on retreat. It was a memorable and formative year for all involved, with significant fruit - including two weddings!

Mark, Chris and extended family did so well, putting up with us extra five. Our daughter, Hannah found a good buddy in their daughter, Jenny, who was the same age. Our oldest, Marc, started school in Junior High and Tim went into the final year of Elementary school. Typical Marc fitted in like a glove, despite the stark cultural differences. 'The Heights' in Newburgh, where Mark and Chris lived, was a profoundly rundown area with many immigrants from all over, with much desperate poverty and all that goes with it. Police officers, continually patrolling the corridors of the Junior High, was just a reflection of the area. Many folks in the church, including Mark and Chris, had chosen to move into the area, in order to reach the people and make a difference.

After three months with the McGraths we found an apartment to rent. It was great, a place to ourselves, amongst the predominantly hispanic and black part of 'The Heights.'

Part way through the ETP year a retreat was arranged in the 'boonies' of north west Jersey, (short for 'boondarks' - remote and historically wild areas of America). The retreat was three days of devotional teaching from Mark, worship and hours of quiet individual contemplation out in the expansive woods surrounding the cabin.

It was a profoundly significant and painful time for me. The day before I had left for the three day retreat, Sue and I had both come to a stark realisation - Sue was pregnant! Oh no! We had three children already, the perfect number. We were in the States. We'd already heard from others in the church, that at that time, it cost $6,000 for baby delivery with a one night stay in the hospital. No way could we afford that sort of money, which was the very least of it - then there would be everything else that went with being a family, not of five but six! Absolutely no way! To make matters worse at that time, it was looking like our twelve month stay in the States was going to be open-ended.

Out in the loneliness of the woods, during our afternoon periods of contemplation, I was crying out to God. 'There must be a mistake. This can't be right.' I kept it all a secret from the rest of the group. No point sharing what may not even be the case. My desperation only increased the more I thought of all the implications.

I put on a brave face in the group sessions, but felt so vulnerable and broken inside. Begrudgingly, by the end of the retreat, having earnestly been crying out to God and hearing nothing, I faced returning to Sue and having to be 'the man' - strong and assured! Towards the end I was crying out, 'God if this is of you then you're going to have to provide.' As I returned home, my faith and trust level, on a scale of one to a hundred, was teetering between five and six!

When Sue and I had put the kids in bed that night, we talked. We were both at our lowest point. We felt trapped. We had no money saved up. We were living hand to mouth. We were already a family of five and as it was were dependent on the very generous giving of those dear church people. We didn't plan this. Were we to cut and run and return to the UK while Sue could still fly during early pregnancy?

The next morning it was clear to us both. The previous night we'd together cried out to God, 'Help.' Now we were both at peace. Sounds crazy, but it's true. We were well and truly out of our depth; we recognised there was nothing else we could do but trust Him; give the panicking over to him. He must have things to show us through all this.

ETP continued to go brilliantly, with lasting relationships building and practical experience in reaching out to non Christians. A challenging highlight was the weekly visit to the County Jail to spend time, one to one, with the inmates.

Later that year, the team spent a very special couple of weeks working with various churches in the UK, though Sue and I stayed back in the US.

The Perfect Number!

Surprise, surprise. God was overwhelmingly faithful. Big time. Because of the 'Student Status' on my visa, we would only have to pay a small fraction of the normal birthing costs. Sue did so well and the hospital care was exemplary with the birth going so well. The McGraths were wonderfully supportive, along with the rest of the church.

It was a girl! Beth Kate joined us and now we were six! As it turned out, it was, indeed, our perfect number. Our heavenly Father really does know what is best for us. He is trustworthy! Beyond our wildest expectations our heavenly Father provided all that we needed through his ever so generous children in our church family.

It didn't take very long to realise with a flourish that Beth was another truly wonderful gift from our heavenly Father. Different again from the other three wonderful kids!

Chapter 25

Big changes in Newburgh Church

The next few months were filled with one shock surprise after another.

Early in summer, Mark announced that he and the family were leaving the church after ten years, to start a new work in central New Jersey, which had been the stamping ground for both Mark and Chris in their early years. I was to act as interim leader, until the new pastor arrived from the UK in the autumn.

At that time, Sue and I had come to the strong conviction that we would not be moving back to the UK after our twelve months were up. There was a small group of folk in the church who regularly made the twenty mile journey to be a part of the church life in Newburgh. We were getting to know them and felt that, when Mark's replacement arrived, we would move out to Middletown, where these folk lived, in order to start a small group and build church with the people in that area.

Roger Brotherton and his wife and daughter, had agreed to move over from the UK to take on the leadership of the Newburgh Church, now that Mark had moved south.

Summer Conference

Every summer there was a week long family conference for all the churches in the family of churches. It was a great first experience for us as a family. The venue was a university campus in the far north of New York State, not far from the Canadian border. The facilities were fantastic, for all the family, with all food provided, and plenty of it. Times of excellent teaching from the teachers in the churches and of course the opportunity to visit Toronto and the Niagara Falls and experience a thorough wetting on the Maid of the Mist, taking us behind the falls, with all the accompanying shrieks of cold delight.

For that year's Family Conference, as in previous years, the main leader of the church in Truro and his wife were in attendance. One afternoon, with no little trepidation, Sue and I shared with them what were now our plans. Having been away for one year at this point, we felt that to be absent from the Truro church for any longer demanded that I resign from eldership. Both Sue and I felt our decision was not up for debate; so we were totally taken aback when our request to resign was flatly rejected. I tried to make the case that I needed to be released as I couldn't fulfil any meaningful responsibility and that negated what I felt was the whole significance of church eldership. We were totally shocked, but there was nothing that could be said. However, the leader did agree that the church's financial support for us would cease.

For the previous twelve months I'd had a measure of involvement with the Truro church from afar. I'd been able to visit a couple of times and had combined my time with the church and also catching up with the shop we had left behind. I had fitted in attending the main trade buying events during my visits. I'd also received a copy of the church monthly accounts. From that summer conference onwards, we received no further communication at all in relation to the church. Added to this, our twelve month's visa now having expired meant that, while applying for a new one, none of us could leave the USA and then re-enter.

A Delightful Discovery

I had quickly cottoned on to the significance of the recently launched new computer that Mark had. It was early days for such things. Being amazingly portable, it went into a shoulder bag and everywhere Mark went. In contrast to one that my brother-in-law had showed me some years before, it looked so easy to use. Surely, even I could use it? When Mark was out of the office he permitted me to use it. Then a great idea. Why not print a weekly church news sheet? One of the programmes on Mark's Apple Macintosh was a copy of the very first 'page layout' software. It was very rudimentary and not easy to control, but it worked. It even pre-dated a competitor soon to reach the market- 'Pagemaker'. When Beth was born, I was amazingly given a gift of $1,000! I saw an ad from a catholic priest in the next town who had a Mac for sale, as he was upgrading, and was asking exactly $1,000. I snapped it up - with Sue's permission of course! Word went round of what I was getting up to.

Not long after, I was invited to join the churches' Apostolic Team. I was also invited to fill the role managing the production of the monthly teaching magazine that circulated among the churches and further afield. It was a long drive, two days a week, down to the office in central

New Jersey with my trusty Macintosh computer, in its bag! The financial support was a great blessing though.

In the autumn we moved into a house to rent in Middletown, twenty miles west of Newburgh. Our plan was to work together with the core group there to build a new church in the town. We also got places in schools for the boys and Hannah just at the start of the new academic year. It was not the easiest of times for the boys as they had to adjust to new schools and start, once again to make new friends. For Hannah it wasn't so bad; this was her first introduction to the elementary school system, which was just the same for the local kids of her age.

Now we could give our attention to building relationships with the Middletown folk and getting to know our new neighbours.

Moving South, New Jersey

Sadly, the year before, the largest of the family of churches in Bergen County, New Jersey, had imploded. Due to the financial 'irregularities' and excessive control from the elders, there was virtually nothing left of the main church of 300 plus folk and the churches planted in Vermont and London.

There was a small group of a dozen or so, who bravely were starting again. They were mainly mature Christians and had been able to stay clear of the earlier excesses. They had pleaded with Ray, the main leader of the family of churches, to help them start afresh in their area of central New Jersey. Subsequently Ray approached Sue and I, strongly encouraging us to change track, as we were still in the early months at Middletown.

Chapter 26

Starting Church Again

Sue and I were now in a real dilemma. We had been building such encouraging relationships with a really good bunch of folks in Middletown. To desert them now would be heart-breaking. What to do? The argument was, 'they still have the opportunity to revert back to where they had been, as part of the Newburgh church, and they now would have a really good pair of Brits: Roger with his wife and daughter who had taken Mark's place.'

Eventually we came round to it. The peace we had, on yet another change of direction, turned to a conviction that it was the right thing to do. We would have to wait until the school year was up and our year's house rental came to an end before we moved. It was so painful sharing all this with the Middletown Group and both Sue and I felt so bad about it. Having let the cat out of the bag, it seemed best to make the change effective at the end of the month. I continued my commute from Middletown to the office in central Jersey two days a week, to work on the family of churches magazine. After my Wednesday in the office I stopped off for the evening meeting with the new group of folk who were continuing their fresh start in Bergen County, New Jersey. On Sundays, we as a family drove down to be with the new group for the day. Surprisingly, something special was happening among us as we sought to deal with some of the pain and disillusionment of the previous church, one person at a time. Quickly, more folk joined us and soon we had to find a Sunday meeting place.

In August we rented and moved south to Washington Township, central New Jersey, across the river from Manhattan. More new schools for the kids - the third in three years. Not easy for British teenagers in affluent east coast USA! Hannah, our oldest girl, was just at the right age and she took it all in her stride, as if it was quite natural; those early days in the school system were easy for her. Her broad American accent was a no brainer, she was quite at home and thrived. Marc, now attending High School, in his mid-teens also seemed to adjust and went with the flow. The area was such a big contrast to Newburgh's poverty, drug, drink and gang culture. The new issue was the affluence and all the expectations that went with it. It was only recently, in conversation with Marc all these years later, that he expressed how hard and pressured it had been for him to cope during that time. Typical Marc - at the time he'd covered it up so well or, maybe as parents, we were just too insensitive?

For Tim it was a completely different matter. Never one to 'just fit in' and go with the flow if he didn't agree. He refused to speak the lingo in the American way - British and proud of it. He connected with a fellow sufferer who was a Chinese immigrant, one friend he'd made who was going through the same as him. Junior High was definitely not a walk in the park for Tim. The cost began to show in his health - he put on a lot of weight and became reclusive at home. Sue and I were getting seriously worried.

Things grew at a surprising rate in the new church and we planned for a 'Church Launch', going public in Ramsey

High School buildings, where we were now meeting on Sundays. We ran a telephone contacting campaign, followed up with information mailings in the area, inviting people to join us. That new venue went so well for us, the Sunday meetings and also the mid-week home gatherings.

The months went by. For both Sue and I, the highlights were the relationships we were building with such a wide variety of people. Folk began to discover Jesus; there were baptisms - the swimming pool in the garden of one of the leaders was great - followed by lots of barbecued food and sunshine! We were attracting a wide demographic from across the surrounding townships. Our central location was ideal - so many millions of people in such close proximity, and we were in the perfect location, adjacent to Paramus, the intersection of the main roads into New York City, westwards and north and south.

We did so many of the 'American things' during those years. While still in Newburgh we had joined with a gang of the Newburgh church men and driven down to Yankee Stadium for a whole new experience: watching American Baseball in the Bronx. We got our monies worth as the game went all the way to the eighth inning and a very late return home.

When living in New Jersey, Sue and I went to the NFL Basketball in Madison Square Gardens. It was fascinating to watch the enthusiasm of the two teams' supporters; that was at least half of the entertainment. Flushing Meadows, in the early evening sunshine, watching the men's singles tennis semi-finals, was also a delight. However, the most scary, was sitting in the second row from the front, watching the ice hockey. The ice puck was moved around at amazing speed and often took flight out of the rink, heading for us cheering onlookers, most times being just restrained from hitting us by the flimsy looking netting; that didn't stop the automatic reaction of ducking, just in case!

After an initial failure at obtaining our Green Card (the visa with right to remain in the US) we took advise. The church leaders agreed to pay for a lawyer to make an application that would 'tick all the boxes', so that we would be able to remain and, also once again, free us up to visit the UK and catch up with family, friends and the church there.

Bolt from the Blue

There was so much encouragement in our lives and the church in Bergen County until (and this indelibly printed on my memory and etched into my psyche) the arrival of two letters. Two days apart, we received separate letters from two of our close friends back in Truro. We had heard earlier, how well it had been going, people becoming Christians and the life of the church vibrant with health. The number attending had gone up and small groups had been multiplying into neighbouring towns. However, recently we had heard nothing at all from the church for many months.

Some while before, we had been shocked to hear that the new third elder we had left behind had had a heart attack; he was recovering and had stepped back from eldership and leading his large accountancy business. He was so young too; nowhere near the age when a heart attack might be an issue. It meant that the main elder was now on his own - but there were lots of good mature Christians to support him.

Now these two letters; we later found out that the writers had no knowledge that the other was also writing to us. What a total bombshell. Many people, good people we knew well, had left the church. More were teetering on the brink. A state of confused division had taken over. In fact, the two families represented by these letters, had just left too. They said that they could not bear it any longer. I was speechless! It was incomprehensible! Sue joined me in my horror and disbelief. How could this be? Surely, it had all been going so well.

The next day we made a phone call to the UK and spoke to one the letter writers. They were mature Christians who we knew, were not prone to flights of fancy. They hadn't taken their decision to leave lightly. They told us more of what had been happening, being careful not to bad-mouth anyone. Apparently trouble had been cooking for some time, bad decisions had been made at the top; relationships had suffered; trust had been irreparably damaged; so many good people had left. The die seemed to be cast. The inevitable was getting closer!

We rang off totally distraught. The list of people who had left seemed endless, many of them we knew so well; they were mature folk, with a passion for Jesus and his kingdom. So many of them were close friends, trusted and loved.

Sue and I knew what we had to do. Those few years in New Jersey had been wonderful. God had provided and lives had been changed for the good, some dramatically. But we were not indispensable!

Chapter 27

Back to UK Heartbreak

We arrived back in Truro at the end of that summer. We found the state of Christian Community Church and the people was even worse than we had anticipated. More people had moved on. There was so much to try to understand and catch up with.

John, a wise and experienced Christian, had been drawn into the leadership team. As my request to resign from eldership previously had been rejected, I was still received as an elder when we returned. It was agreed by the three of us, that Mark in the States, should help us in finding the way forward.

I set about contacting so many of my good friends who had left the church and meeting up to listen to their stories. Sadly, there was a common thread running through most of the painful stories and strong emotions were expressed; all the time I was asking myself the same question, 'What on earth is the way forward, Father?' There were still some sixty folk remaining, so there was all to play for.

It was only looking back, years later, that I began to realise that I was being confronted, big time; here was this 'Big C' once again, 'Control'! As it turned out, control was to make itself known even more, further down the road.

The three of us had weekly transatlantic 'phone meetings with Mark. As the weeks passed the picture became clearer, to me at least. We agreed together that Mark had to come and pay us a visit as soon as possible. In the first week of January Mark joined us for a week or so - it was so much easier to talk turkey, face to face. A meeting with the current church folk was arranged for the next week. Mark presented his conclusion - the founding leader needed to step back and Mark would take things forward from there. On the spot, the founding leader made his response quite clear. He insisted that he must stay in charge. There was nothing more that could be said. For a significant number of those attending, that was their last meeting at Truro Community Church. Sue and I, with very heavy hearts, left as well. Mark returned to the US, ending his involvement of over almost ten years. The church continued for another few years before it finally wound up.

Another New Church - Kings Church Cornwall

For those who'd now left, there didn't seem to be any alternative in Cornwall for folk who were committed and passionate for local church and what God seemed to be doing, at that time, across the rest of the country. As the months passed and summer was on us, word was filtering through; a bunch of six families, plus children, had felt a call from God to leave where they were in north Yorkshire and start a new church in west Cornwall - the end of the earth! We also heard they were now gathering on a Sunday in a school in Penzance.

Finally, in September, Sue and I thought we would go and check it out; we had nothing to lose, despite the long drive all the way from Truro to Penzance. What we found was amazing. There were more than thirty people, adults and children, and we were saying 'Oh, there's such and such, and there, and there,' people we knew from previous church experiences. Also there were several folk from the church we had recently left doing the same as us, spying out the land. The time of praise and worship was enthusiastic and Jesus centred. We heard tongues being used and the prophetic was happening. There was a real sense of freedom and life about the whole thing; towards the end someone stood and shared teaching from the Bible with enthusiasm and authority. Afterwards there were coffees and teas, with time catching up with past friends and finding out from those who were obviously the leading characters, what they were all about; where they'd come from and where they were looking to go.

We got into our car for the sixty minute drive back home. 'Well, that was interesting, Sue.' I said, as we set off. 'Yes indeed,' she replied. 'Maybe we should visit again. What do you think kids?' 'Yeah, why not?' came the reply. Within the month, it became a regular Sunday journey for us.

The new Kings Church grew rapidly. Several families and singles who had grown up in the Exclusive Brethren had joined the church from the beginning. They'd been forced out and shunned by their families when they were baptised in the Spirit, they had spoken in tongues and experienced the Holy Spirit making Jesus real to them in a truly transformational way. There was now a whole bunch of us from our previous church in Truro that were a part of this new church. It was evident that the leading person was Joff Day. Joff was clearly gifted in teaching, was a natural leader and visionary, with experience in the family of churches of which he and the others from Yorkshire had been a part.

Rapid Growth

As the months moved into years the church grew amazingly. The Sunday gathering moved to a school in Redruth with excellent facilities and was much better for the whole western area of Cornwall that were now being served. People were experiencing father God in so many surprising ways. Other folk of all ages were experiencing salvation for the first time and many were exercising various gifts of the Spirit. Praise and worship grew in breadth and depth. Small groups were established in all the main towns of central and west Cornwall as people were hungry for more of God. Sue and I took on the responsibility for leading one of the small groups.

Chapter 28

Strange 'Heart Surgery' Begins!

Arriving at this stage in our life was far from our desires or expectations. The previous couple of years had been so tumultuous for us two and our four children.

Re-entry from living and leading church in the USA, then the disintegration of the church that had released us to the States in the first place, was an almost overwhelming heartbreak; plus the stark contrast of re-integration into UK schools for our kids, especially for the one that now had a broad New Jersey twang!

Along with a number of good friends from the previous church, as a family we quickly adapted to this new expression of church. It was so good to be with so many people who were really enthusiastic for knowing and experiencing more of Jesus and how he wanted us to grow and change. It was full of life, great praise and worship, and open to what God was doing through his Holy Spirit. And he did.

There was a new expression of prayer, praise, worship and the gifts of the Spirit. Without doubt, we were experiencing a whole new 'wind' of the Spirit of God blowing through us.

Many people were being set free from issues in their lives they had never even realised were there. Sin was being dealt with, people were experiencing a release and intimacy with God, like never before. The prophetic was taking on a completely new meaning and relevance in people's lives.

What's happening in me, what's it about?

It was so strange! A point came, whenever we gathered together on a Sunday or during the week and even on my own, that something happened within me - no matter what was going on around me. As I started to praise, clap and exalt Jesus, our amazing God, I just had to be on the floor, flat on my back and tears would stream from my eyes; there were no chairs in the way, so that helped! Time after time, the same thing - flat on my back, tears streaming, crying to God, my father: 'Soften my heart Lord, soften my heart.' Time didn't seem to matter; I was in his presence.

And so it went on. Weeks ran into months, months to several years. Always the same - flat on my back, the same cry, the tears flowing . . . with the added question, 'What is this all about Lord?' Seemedly, no answer was forthcoming. There was one reassuring thought though - I didn't feel that I was a particularly 'odd bod', as God was doing all sorts of things with others around me. The reality was, I felt I was co-operating whole-heartedly with what I was sure about, my Father was doing things deep within me. I had such a sense, feeling and experience of his presence and intimacy during those times.

As time passed, my question, 'What's this about Lord?' was not answered but to my agonising cry, 'Soften my heart, Lord, soften my heart' was added, 'Break my heart Lord, with what breaks yours.' The weeping continued and over the weeks I felt the increased intensity of my pleading. I went with it, 'If this is all of you Father, though I'm not feeling much softer of heart, I'll trust you're doing something.

Those months left a deep impression on me and, definitely, I was different as a result. My heavenly Father had started a process, deep within me, that only years later I would begin to understand and start to come into the good of. I have kept all of this to myself and it all sounds a bit weird.

Fascinatingly, these weird and wonderful things were not just limited to the wild west English County of Cornwall. During this time, word was now filtering through of what God was also doing in Toronto, Canada. It was the mid 1990s and soon we were hearing of all sorts of different new expressions of God's life. Signs and wonders were taking place amongst Christians across all denominations in the UK and across the globe.

Even now as I write, sitting on a bench looking across the vast harbour in front of me, full of boats, I'm overwhelmed with weeping and wonder; the cry of my heart back then, is still a daily cry, to this day. 'Soften my heart, Lord, soften my heart, break my heart, Lord with what breaks yours.' Our wonderful Father God has so much more to reveal in the years ahead. This period was just a stepping stone into so much more he has for his church and his world, that is in such desperate need. As the world gets darker, the light will shine even brighter!

Chapter 29

A Painful Lesson

Sue was a wonderful, caring person. That had to be the reason she'd trained as a nurse, straight out of school. She was gentle, related so well with people and had a consummate servant's heart. Of course I am totally biased but, I saw and experienced the benefit of who she was in so many wonderful ways. What a privilege to have Sue as my wife and mother to our children.

This caring heart of hers was the reason she jumped at the opportunity, when a Phillipi Trust Counselling training course locally, became available. She pursued the course whole heartedly for two years and thrived on it. After working nights in a local care home, she grasped the opportunity of the specialised work in the local Women's Centre. It was her caring heart that made it natural to befriend Lynda, one of the mums, with her toddler, who was attending the same toddler group as Sue with Beth, our youngest. The two kids hit it off and the mums did what the mums do at these groups - they chatted.

Lynda had been brought up attending her local parish church. It was so natural that they would talk together about Jesus. Over the months, Sue supported Lynda through the relational turmoil that seemed to be so much of her life. She now had a new boy friend, with the hope of better things. They got married in the parish church and a while later a baby boy was born.

I guess it was obvious, given the relationship that had been built, that Sue and I were invited to be God-parents at the forth coming christening. That was a real poser for Sue and I. Though I had been christened as a baby, we both felt that, while we wanted to support both the parents as much as we could, in all conscience we couldn't act as God parents. It would be counter to everything that Sue had been sharing with Lynda; water baptism followed the individual personal choice to accept Jesus' sacrifice and choose him as Lord of our life. We did, however, say that we would express our support of them by attending the ceremony.

Big Surprise

On the Monday morning after the christening, which was my day off, Sue and I got a phone call from one of the Kings Church elders. The elders wanted to meet up with us both; they would come to our house that afternoon. Well, that was unusual - all three of them.

We were all sat in our lounge. The whole experience is indelibly imprinted on my mind and engraved in my feelings. Joff came straight to the point. They had heard the reason for our non-attendance at the Sunday meeting the day before. We had attended a christening. How could we possibly do such a thing when we knew of the very clear view on baptism held and preached by the elders. It wasn't actually a question, but an indignant statement. Sue and I were both totally gobsmacked! Joff continued. It would be impossible for them to endorse us; we were taken out of home group leadership with immediate effect; the final few sessions of the weekly pastoral training course I was running for the group leaders, was cancelled. With that, they stood up. We saw them to the door.

Sue and I were in total shock. Incredulity. How they had carried on; what they had said and they didn't even ask us for any justification we might have had for our actions. Please! For Sue and I it was not the ceremony that it was about. It was our care and support for the dear, needy people that we were both involved with. We felt violated.

The next few days were excruciating. God had done and was continuing to do amazing things in this church and through the people there. There were definitely some excesses in places, but that didn't take away from the life-changing things that God had been and was still doing amongst us all by his Spirit. Surely, we would have to leave and cut our ties; that was so obviously the right thing to do but, there was a nagging feeling deep down that we both felt. It seemed so irrational, but we had no peace in our decision to leave. We lived with it over the next few days and, gradually, something else, that we also believed, was emerging. We both felt God was showing us at a deep level, what his heart was for us, in this situation.

But how could we possibly submit to the elders in this and continue as if nothing had happened? The agony got even worse through the sleep disturbed nights. However, this ridiculous thought to stay, grew to a conviction. Heavenly Father, if this is what you want for us, you are going to have to change our hearts. It has to be real for us, or it would just be a legalistic show and pretence.

It seemed strange, but I wondered if this be the first significant 'test' of the state of my heart - not my head? Maybe the issue of the moment was not the correctness or otherwise of the elders. A wild thought; maybe God's heart is breaking so much when he sees what his children do or, maybe, don't do. Wonderfully for us all he doesn't throw a tantrum and insist on rightness, but graciously accepts us, warts and all; a breaking heart, but still loving - Jesus bore it all! By the end of that week we had peace - pain, but peace. It was the right thing to do. 'But Father help! If we are to submit to their leadership, in the face of such wrong and gracelessness, it's got to be your Spirit in us, at our heart level.'

For me, this was a whole new and ground-breaking lesson and experience. Maybe this was also going to be a significant factor for us in the days ahead? Will we really trust our heavenly Father?

For us it was a prime opportunity of facing up to another of the 'Big 'Cs' - 'Choice'

We said nothing to anyone. Saturday came and I went along to the regular early morning prayer time in our town with the usual lively format of praise, worship and responding to God, prayer and whichever way He was prompting that morning. I said nothing about our situation of having been 'stepped down' - being 'disciplined.' Maybe I was supersensitive, but I felt there was definitely something in the air; the way people looked at me, but said nothing. The word must have got out and maybe they were embarrassed. It took weeks to begin to feel a bit more normal again; such a painful time, for both of us, but our conviction that it had been right to choose to submit was only strengthening.

Could there be a connection with the strange and puzzling thing God had been doing with me over the last few months? Maybe so. In the days ahead 'maybe so' changed to 'absolutely so!' Definitely my heart was feeling broken. We were moved to another small group and it was a tremendous blessing to get to know David and Jenny Mullinger, the small group leaders. They were such caring and personable people - a timely breath of fresh air. Our relationship with Jenny and David turned out to be very special and lasted for many years.

A Couple of Years Pass

Gradually, Sue and I were being 'rehabilitated,' with the passing of time. I was getting more involved with encouraging the designated pastoral elder. The two of us were beginning to agree on principles and practices for better care for the still enlarging congregation. The months passed.

It was the end of summer and Joff had just returned from his family holiday. After the time of praise and the normal worship session Joff stood to speak. He announced that God had spoken to him while away. It was a word of corrective admonishment: Joff was the pastor of the church and he'd given it over to others. He must take that role back and be it. He announced to the congregation that, as of now, he was going to be doing it.

I was shocked to my core. Everyone knew that Joff was a highly gifted enthusiast for Jesus. Without question he was an outstandingly gifted leader; he was universally seen as that. The one thing he was not, was a pastor. He could be really personable, but a pastor? Definitely not.

The context and the whole scenario was a total shock. There were obviously gifted people through the church who had been developing and functioning; evangelistic, prophetic and caring people. Folk who were being used in healing, deliverance and those with a heart for discipling. There was so much good fruit showing in the church. Many had come to know Jesus and his saving power and there was much tangible evidence of beginning to function as 'a body.'

Finally, Joff told us that, as the primary elder, God had told him that major change had to be implemented; he had not been properly in charge and must take his rightful place as the 'Shepherd'.

The conversation during the thirty minute drive back home that lunch time was about the weather. After lunch when the kids had gone off to play or do homework, Sue and I talked and found we were both on the same page. Absolutely, there was no doubt. Now was the time to leave the church; there was no argument; we both saw the same thing and now had a peace as to the rightness of the decision. It was a peace and conviction that had remained with us when we made an appointment to meet up with Joff and his wife a few weeks later.

It was not a meeting we relished. We both felt so sad to say goodbye, along with the reasons for our leaving. We didn't go into detail, but rather we thanked them whole-heatedly for all that we had learnt and benefited from our time in Kings Church, over the past years, but expressed our conviction that now was the time for us to move on. We were indeed surprised at the shock they both expressed. We bade them farewell.

Ten Years Later

It was some ten years later before I, on my own, had the opportunity of dropping in on them both. It was a significantly poignant time for me, being the first time I'd visited Cornwall for quite a few years. Sue and I had both moved on a lot over that time. The great sadness had remained but, individually, we felt we had come to a place of releasing them from how we had been treated, and felt genuinely free of them; we'd learnt so much through the whole experience at Kings Church.

Joff and Elaine received me very graciously and we had an excellent time catching up. I left feeling really blessed by our time together. Before hand, I'd really wondered how they would receive me. They seemed pleased to see me and that 'issue' in our past relationship never came up. Well done Joff and Elaine, I thought. I climbed into my car, and felt finally a sad chapter had closed for me.

Those intervening ten years had not been easy for Sue and I, or for Joff and Elaine at Kings Church. It had wound down and no longer existed. Their kids had now grown and moved away and, as a couple, they were now moving away from Cornwall.

Chapter 30

Another one of the 'Big Cs'
'Choice'

It was quite a few years ago now, but it made a deep impression on me at the time, another which is indelibly printed in my psyche! In the early days of our time living in the US, as a family, we went for a day out with our good friends Mark and Chris, to the the 'Big City' - New York. The plan was to go up those, now absent, Twin Towers. Gazing up at their height from the road below was an awesome experience. They were so impressive. The lift felt like take off at Cape Canaveral - was it going to stop at the top? It did, but my stomach arrived a fair bit later than I did!

What made the Twin Towers so extra special was their standing only about five metres apart. There was a real treat two floors below the top floor restaurant. There was a corridor that joined both towers, so we could walk from one to the other, right at the top. Great idea. The walls of the corridor on both sides were made of glass, so we could see New York through both sides. Then a really smart idea - the floor was all one piece of glass. The view to left and right was totally ignored. There I was, standing at the edge of the walkway, looking down. It was such a very long drop. The people on the ground below seemed like ants scuttling around, five hundred and forty metres below and my stomach began churning and the adrenaline pumping. Our boys pushed past me and ran across, laughing at their dad then, from the other side, pointing and tittering at me.

My mind was racing as I stood on the edge, pretending that I was admiring the view, but, in reality, processing my dilemma. I knew that it must be safe, but the kids were lighter than me: surely they wouldn't allow people across if there was any mortal danger: they would have their socks sued off.

Finally, now feeling a total coward, I made the decision: I made the choice: I stepped out into space and walked across. There was only one further thing I had to do - walk back again. That was now easy, but I still had to make the choice. Issue solved.

Mark and Chris had agreed that we would meet up after this in the restaurant with the outside circular viewing platform. We all had coffee or soft drinks; they'd done all this before, so they explained what was now happening to us in the restaurant. 'We're moving, look out of the windows.' Oh my, yes, we are moving. The whole floor was rotating ever so slowly. What an idea, just looking out of the window we could see the whole 360 degree panorama taking place in front of us. Totally gob smacking!

What memories of that day remained. Needless to say, what made the deepest impact on me, was that glass walkway. One way or other I had to make that choice as I stood on the brink. What a great practical illustration. After all the reasoning, weighing the pros and cons, taking into account the emotional drives and feelings, the inevitable result has to be a choice. One way or the other, we have to make a choice - no choice is in fact a choice!

The Bible book of Genesis gives us the record that the man and the woman were both equipped to make choices, in a way that nothing else in all of creation could. The two options were presented along with the consequences: have what you've got now or loose it. You are equipped to choose.

'The Lord God took the man and put him in the garden of Eden to work it and keep it.
And the Lord God commanded the man, saying, 'You may surely eat of every tree of the garden,
but of the tree of the knowledge of good and evil you shall not eat, for in the day that you eat of it you shall surely die.''
(Genesis 1vv15-17)

What an awesome privilege we have that we can make choices. However, having to make a choice often feels so difficult and even burdensome, when confronted with having to make a choice between different options. The truth of the matter is that our Creator set mankind apart from the rest of creation and gave us this wonderful gift! We can reason, weigh options, asses emotions and feelings, follow the route we've been taught, submit to habit, or even choose not to make a choice, which of course is also a choice! At the end of every day we have made so many choices! Most definitely a 'Big C'.

There is also another significant part of 'faith' - Action!

Chapter 31

Yet More Testing Emerging

Real Life Church

Yet another one of those change points! Such disappointment and disillusion with yet another church. Maybe, it was time to walk away from all this church stuff? But how could I walk away from what was a deep passion within me? I was progressively realising that God had sown a seed within me, which had been growing through all the painful experiences Sue and I had already been through. It was also dawning on me that not all was hunky-dory, with me. Maybe, there needed to be profound change in me also.

Wonderfully, we met up with Bill and Betty, good friends from years before, in a church in which Sue and I had both been a part. We seemed to be looking in the same direction. Both Bill and Betty were so different from much we had known in the past - they were so 'relational,' caring, and real! They were a breath of fresh air for both Sue and I, along with our two girls, Hannah and Beth, who were still at home with us. It didn't take long before others were connecting and we had to find somewhere to meet. Fascinatingly, many of the folk that joined with us were definitely needy people, or rather, they were going through things which were causing them to connect to their neediness. To be in a caring environment was so good.

Shock Diagnosis

It was during this time that Sue, still in her mid-forties, was noticing a significant limp in one of her legs. The GP arranged for some tests. A week or so later, we both went to the hospital for the test results. The diagnosis: Sue had Parkinson's Disease. A death warrant was issued. Life was going to change, for both Sue and I, along with Hannah approaching mid-teens and Beth, not yet in her teens.

Can it really be?

I am totally convinced and more so, as the years have passed and one thing has led to another; connecting with the many mistakes I've made and recognising the seemingly blind alleys I've walked down only leads me to the certainty of my conviction.

The Apostle Paul was spot on when he wrote to the Roman church, 'I'm convinced, that in all things, God works together for the good, for all those who are called according to his purposes.' (Romans 8:28). If this is not true in practice, then there are only a few other options open to us:

1. The whole of life is down to chance!

2. I am the master of my own destiny. If life is tough, it's down to me to change it. Success or failure is up to me.

3. t's all a matter of fate. If there is some kind of a divine power that set it all in motion, then now it's up to each creature to make the most of it.

What the passing of the years has demonstrated for me, over and over, is the total inadequacy of all these and many other different world views. They all have one thing in common - ultimately they all lead to fatalistic despair.

What the loving, all powerful, creator God revealed through the life of Jesus, two thousand years ago, can be the only explanation. For Sue and I, what seemed to be the random, unconnected events and experiences that we had lived through turned out to be the many disparate strands, weaving a truly wonderful and multicoloured tapestry, by a hand not our own.

Looking back, I can see it so clearly. Many of the decisions we had made seemed to end in blind alleys, with such disappointment, pain and failure, even disillusionment.This following Jesus seemed to be so hard and definitely not 'just a walk in the park.'

However, in retrospect, it's become so clear to me that my amazing heavenly Father has been shaping me, changing me radically, softening me and building into me a strong and certain conviction of hope. I'm totally convinced: He is working in all these things for the very best.

Chapter 32

Only God Could Be in This

Sunrise and Sunrise Software - God's Fingerprints

For the longest time I had been convinced that being supported by a church was a low priority for Sue and I. There were seasons when we were supported by the church we were in but, being able to be fully involved with my passion for church, while being self supporting, was the route for much of our married life.

My work situation had been fast changing since we came back from the States. Over the years away in the States, Pete had done a great job of managing the shop. Coming back coincided with the current shop lease expiring in a few months. It clearly was not time to call it a day. Sunrise had been doing excellently in it's prime location in the town with a staff of five full-timers and other part-timers. We relocated to a new site with larger floor space.

Times were changing. The next generation Macintosh computer I'd obtained in the States and the page layout software I'd mastered then, were proving so useful in so many ways. While away I'd also invested in a Bible software package for the Mac. It was great.

I'd had a conversation with an Australian Christian business man in Truro, one day in the shop, which was the trigger. I told him about the Bible software programme that I had. Though mine was for the Mac computer, I mentioned that I knew there was an early Windows Bible software package available in the US; I agreed to get it for him. That was the start of Sunrise Software, which was run from our basement stock room and office space under our new shop location!

Following this, I contacted the Christian book publishers and music companies that supplied us in the shop. None had heard of such a thing as the Bible and commentaries being available for the computer.

Then I had a wild thought. Why not contact some of the main companies in the US and see if they would sell to me. By their response it was obviously a novel idea for them too - but why not? There seemed no sense in my trying to wholesale to the other UK Christian bookshops at that time surely it would be a very hard sell. But as they were not interested, why don't I try to advertise in the UK Christian magazines and denominational newspapers? If there was any response, I could put together product information with my page layout software and print it out on the laser printer; the customer could pay by cheque and then I could post the package off to them. Direct selling was hardly heard of at that time.

I started off with a small ad in one of the weekly Christian denominational papers. By that time I'd risked it and had bought in a few Bible packages. Following the first ad and a phone call, I had the first sale - nearly two hundred pounds worth. Mega!

That first order was so exciting. The interest was there, more orders followed and trips to the post office began to be a daily experience.The range expanded; soon we were distributing six US suppliers - the business was nearly all for Windows, which was now moving to Version 3. But, I was still loyal to my first love: we had the one available Mac programme at that time. I was still managing the shop upstairs, but due to what was now happening downstairs, we took on another full-timer Phil, a great salesman and asset on the shop floor. Now it was also necessary for a part-time bookkeeper.

Exciting Developments

Several years later, the pressure of the two businesses, along with the increasing software developments, all the responsibilities had rested on Sue and I. We both agreed it was time to look for a new owner for the shop and to find separate premises for Sunrise Software in order to continue to expand it. 'If you are in this Father, You're going to have to fit it all together.' We told the staff of our intention.

A week or so later Pete told me that his brother, who managed a Christian bookshop in another Cornish town, was interested in buying, on behalf of the Christian organisation that owned his shop. There was so much interest, that soon we were talking of a purchase price. Where would we operate the software business from? There wouldn't be very much money left, after we'd paid back the loan we had on the current shop premises. Once again, it all seemed a crazy journey. In a very real way it felt easy to trust our heavenly Father we had no alternative! However, that didn't make trusting any less of an on-going challenge. Were our motives right? Was it just our 'good idea', my egoism and foolishness?

The day we signed the solicitor's papers there was absolutely no room for doubt. Once again, so patently, God's hand was in it. I vacated the shop premises, said farewell to Pete and the staff, piled my computer, printer and software stock into the car and drove the few hundred yards down the road to climb the steep stairs to the new, second floor, two roomed office on Old Bridge Street, Truro. It was small but would do myself and the bookkeeper just fine for a start. One room was the office and the other was the stock and 'shipping' room. Oh yes, the bookkeeper had agreed to continue doing mornings running the new office bookkeeping.

There was now no let up creating and printing out the growing product catalogues for the ever increasing range of programmes and packages we were carrying. It wasn't just us, the market in the US was expanding phenomenally. New companies in the market were offering more and more Bible translations, study aids and commentaries. Ending each day in the Post Office now was a permanent date, but I was coping.

One morning I answered the 'phone. The caller said his name was Andy, we'd not met, but he would like to drop by and have a chat. He sounded normal enough, so I agreed. He came that afternoon. He'd not long been married and he and his wife had moved to Cornwall, for his new job working with a local wind turbine company. Sadly, after a few months that business had collapsed. He was a Christian, had a university degree with computer skills and he believed he might be able to help with Sunrise Software.-. would I give him a try?

I probed, questioned and explained a bit of our history, what we were doing and where I thought we were going. I also mentioned that we weren't able to pay a lot.He didn't seem to be put off. We left it there and I said I would give him a call the next day. That evening I shared it all with Sue, expressing my doubts, money being the main one; we couldn't afford him. She had been sitting opposite with a broad grin as I'd related the meeting.

'Wonderful,' she exclaimed at the end of all my negativeness. 'Grab him, and trust God!' she added. Darn it! Sue was voicing exactly what I'd been feeling, right from the start of my time with Andy, that afternoon. This had to be a God thing. And so it proved to be in so many different ways. Andy started full time two weeks later. Now we were two and a half, but not for long. Lesley, someone we knew from a previous church, also joined us to work mornings. She did a great job managing the dispatch of the orders. Now we were three! How wonderful is the hand of our heavenly Father; even when we've questioned and doubted! The sales continued to grow with the extra work and the income. Wonderfully, we were meeting all our financial commitments. Maybe I needed to learn about this 'doubt' thing?

It wasn't just the mail order business that was making fresh demands. A growing number of Christian events were taking place up and down the country. The Christian Computer Association wanted us to exhibit and demonstrate our software. Their events usually were for two days over a weekend; they were held from Scotland down to all areas of the British Isles. Financially they were well worth the effort. Sue gracefully put up with my absences. As the weeks passed, the christian bookshops were also beginning to catch on, as more people were expecting them to be stocking Christian software. Where to now? Andy and I were stretched to the limit. Andy had also taken on the production of our own clip art packages; with the availability of computers and printers, church magazines were experiencing a whole new existence. All good, but we had no more space to take on the now glaring need for more staff. The answer was obvious, and what a gem Andy had turned out to be; in the years ahead he became a mainstay of the business.

Chapter 33

Ups and Downs

Even More Expansion

We moved into our new two unit office in Scorrier with plenty of room to expand; one unit for the office and the other for stock and dispatch. From here on everything just grew rapidly. Within a year or so we were employing twelve people; with a retail sales rep travelling the UK, an order department, customer technical support, graphic designer and more. Eventually, we were the only distributor into the UK Christian market; other single product distributors had ceased trading.

The demands on demonstrating and selling at the multitude of Christian events now taking place throughout the year, meant more time was being spent travelling the nation. For me now, the annual ten day trip to the US, for the huge Christian Booksellers Convention was essential, enabling us to continue building relationships with our many suppliers.

There was so much to thank our heavenly Father for; the doors he'd opened were amazing, along with the employment opportunities we were able to provide. So much of what we were now doing was directly connected to those years we'd spent in the US and also to the experiences gained through our Sunrise shop. We passed our half million pound turnover and the numbers continued to rise. Needs must, our office increased to four units, with wonderful experienced staff in their different roles.

Then a concept, that was quite new to me, joined my vocabulary - we were 'overtrading'. Our own products were just a small proportion of our massive sales. Often the lead time for most of our Bible related products from order to delivery to us from the US, was four to six weeks. Because of the volume of our sales demanding a 24 hour turn around at our end and the supplies to shops being on monthly terms, at the best, we were paying for an increasing amount of stock well before we received payment. We had never had capital investment in the company.

Dramatic Business Developments

The Managing Director of the largest UK book distributors and also the nationwide chain of Wesley Owen Christian bookshops, was expressing interest in us. Evidently we had come to the attention of the man that counted. The company, STL, was based in Carlisle with a warehouse and office staff of over 700, along with growing interests in the US. The Managing Director made a suggestion - that we partner with them! They would do our distribution through their warehouse and also could easily take on our accounts through their large accounts department. We could save on some staff costs and along with the efficiency of their 24 hour stock turn, it would be of significant benefit to us. They would charge just a small percentage when products had been invoiced or money taken. It would significantly improve our cash flow. To make it work, we would need to form a Limited Company, to safeguard all involved. The Managing Director had a suggestion; he strongly recommended a retired Christian businessman who would make an excellent chairman. We now had much food for thought.

After several meetings with the Managing Director and Finance Director of STL, much thought and chatting with our staff, along with the invaluable wisdom of Andy's dad, who was a senior partner in a large accountancy firm, a decision was arrived at. We went for it. Andy, Rick and I became the directors with Gordon, a lovely Scot and a retired businessman, who would be the chairman; Janet the STL Finance Director became our Company Secretary. The monthly board meetings followed in our offices.

The Cost of Success

Another year or so passed and it was working well. God had so evidently been in the change and even more opportunities opened up. But then came a glitch. Rick had been faithfully travelling the UK and Northern Ireland, selling and supporting our products in the Christian bookshops. But then the rate of sales through some of the shops began to slow and hence the trade orders also began to slow. Three months on there was a definite trend. It was not to be surprised at really, our significant direct selling business to end users was competing with these bookshops. The hardest thing, with heart-wrenching sadness, was having to let Rick go as the business could no longer support him.

Not long after we missed making our monthly payment to STL for their services; and then after two months of defaulting, we were £30,000 in debt to our partners. Eventually, after many 'phone calls and meetings, they put forward a plan to take over the business, at the price of our outstanding debt to them.

There didn't seem to be any other way forward. Over the next few months the plan was executed. The office in Scorrier, Cornwall, would be closed. The staff that wished to transfer to STL would move to Carlisle, but if not, they would be paid redundancy. Andy and I, plus Rob our technical support guy, decided to make the move and did so immediately. while Bob, another colleague and I spent the next month in Carlisle aiding the transition of the business to STL, then travelling back to Cornwall for the weekends. After that first month of the weekly commutes with Bob, his time came to an end and we said our farewells. He then had to look for work back in Cornwall. It was all so gut-wrenchingly sad.

For the next six months I spent alternate weeks working in Carlisle and then from home in Truro. Due to the horrendous motorway traffic I opted to travel the 450 miles each way through the night. If lucky, I had the stars and moon for company, with the nagging opportunity to reflect on the great joy but, also, the sadness of all that had happened over those past months and years, before I finally arrived back home in the small hours of the morning.

They really had been painful months. The agony of having to lay off good and faithful people and trying to come to terms with what seemed to be such failure. How the mighty have fallen! 'Father, where are you in all this? How could you let this happen? Had I made a great big blunder in going in with the big boys? Was it really just a cynical plan, from the beginning, that the Managing Director had to acquire us? How can I trust you God, when I had complete peace over the decision? What an idiot I must be!'

By the beginning of August that year we were ready to move house into rented accommodation, paid for by STL.

That move would give us time to settle and find our own home in Carlisle.

Chapter 34

Crisis - Heart Attack!

Our Truro house was now sold and the removals company was booked for the big move in two weeks time. I was now in Cumbria and it was the Thursday of my last week of commuting, before our house move to Carlisle. Very early that morning the phone rang. My son, Tim, spoke, 'Mum's in hospital. She's had a severe heart attack. She's alive.' Pause for breath. 'Right Tim, I'm on my way, I'll get there just as quickly as I can.' I jumped into the car straight away and drove non-stop, like a bat out of hell, to the Truro hospital.

Sue was awake when I got there later that day. It had been very close. 'It's a dissection of the artery, quite unusual and specially considering she is only in her forties, not overweight and with no previous history.' I was told. 'And, yes, we do need to operate but the specialist heart surgeon has just gone on holiday.'

The next day I met with the consultant neurologist. He was aghast when he saw the level of medication that Sue was on. For these past years this medication level had become essential in order to bring a measure of control for her Parkinson effects. The consultant told me that at these levels of medication Sue would be fitting. I told him Sue had never fitted at all over the months she'd been on this level of cobenyldopas; he obviously felt the need to be responsible and do the right thing. On the spot he modified the dosages to bring them into line with normal practice and instructed the nurse accordingly.

Early the next morning, I visited the hospital to see how she was. I was greeted by a distraught nurse, with Sue in utter panic. She had lost total control of her swallowing and her movement. Sue was in total desperation. The neurologist was summoned - I didn't know what to say. 'You must do something. Please.' In response, he told me to instruct the nurse to get Sue back on to the medication levels she'd been on before. Within the hour Sue was back under control.

After a week, due to the heart specialist still being away for a few more weeks, the neurologist finally decided that Sue should be sent to Cumbria; the Infirmary there probably had the heart surgeons required. A couple of days later, along with a nurse, Sue was driven by ambulance to Carlisle. Four days days later, the girls and I, along with Tim's help, moved north to our new rented accommodation.

Now that Sue was in the Carlisle Infirmary we expected she would have the heart surgery we'd been told she needed. Two weeks passed and the hospital staff remained so very vague. Finally we got a result. Sue could be released forthwith; she had made a good recovery and the stent put into her artery in Truro was working well. She now had extra heart related medications to add to all the Parkinson's medications, so she could go home! As long as she took it easy to start with and built up her strength slowly, there was no reason she could not live and get about normally. Needless to say, she was delighted to be away from all that hospital stuff and into our new rented house. She would be able to support Beth, as she had just started a new year at the secondary school while Hannah was in her first year of sixth form, doing English lit., communication studies and textiles.

The four of us settled quickly into our new home in Carlisle and soon started to look for the right house that we could purchase with the proceeds of our Truro house, with a little help from the mortgage company!

Cornwall to Carlisle in Cumbria, the farthest city of the kingdom; what a profound change in all ways for all four of us. So many adjustments were needed: the geography, the way people talked, definitely the very different weather. Starting again to make friends and build relationships, especially for our two teenage girls, was very tough. We were starting a whole new world, yet again.

Three months later we had our first appointment with the neurologist in Carlisle - a regular check up. At that time the county was without its own specialist neurologist, so a neurologist from Newcastle filled the essential gaps and was available for monthly consultations. A friend, in the church we had now started to attend, warned us, 'I've had to see this man; he's elderly, so austere and not personable at all.' We were prepared. It was to be an indelibly imprinted experience.

An Amazing God Thing

'Diagnosis Parkinson's Disease. Right? Your notes have not come through yet; do you have a list of her medication?' I handed the long list of Sue's medications to him. He read through the list. Something happened. He looked up with a gentle smile towards Sue, for the first time. 'Does it have the required effect?' I replied in the affirmative and added. When the medication was reduced, following her heart attack in Cornwall, the effect on Sue was disastrous.' The gentleman's demeanour had transformed on a sixpence. 'Well m'dear, what we need to do is have you into my ward for a few days, to do some tests.' Sue instantly dissolved into a flood of tears. She couldn't face the prospect of going back into a hospital, after all she had gone through in those previous few months.

'There's no rush, let's leave it for a few months.' He responded with a tender smile. Two months later, the first week in January, I drove Sue across to the Royal Victoria Infirmary in Newcastle, a massive teaching hospital. It had been agreed that it would just be Monday to Friday while they did a few tests. The next evening I visited to see how she was doing. The doctor on the ward explained the way forward. They would start with various tests and then begin to reduce the medication she had been taking.

The next morning, at seven o'clock, Dr Bates, the specialist we had met those two months before in Carlisle, had done his early morning ward rounds. Once again Sue was climbing up the wall. She was panicking big time, struggling to be able to swallow. The specialist had immediately reinstated her medication and Sue was rapidly coming back under control again.

The doctor I was talking to explained the situation. As they had expected, Sue's response to the drug withdrawal had confirmed the diagnosis. Sue did not have Parkinson's Disease! He continued saying that Sue had Multiple System Atrophy. He was one of several consultant neurologists on the team of Professor Bates, who was also on the teaching staff of the Newcastle Medical School. This was his specialist ward, where they were continuing research into a relatively recently isolated disease, also known as Shy-

Dreyer Syndrome, named by the neurologists who had recently isolated it in the States. Professor Bates, the doctor who we'd met in Carlisle those two months before, along with his team in Newcastle, worked for one of very few hospitals in the UK researching into MSA at that time. Friday came, Sue had coped well with the rest of the week, but was so relieved to be back home.

The consequences of this diagnosis had such a profound impact on the months and years that followed. The support that was now provided at this stage, began to make a profound difference in the home, as Sue's functionality slowly deteriorated. We discovered the differences between Parkinson's Disease and Multiple System Atrophy. It was very tough information to accept. Any and all of the autonomic bodily systems could be affected by this neurological deterioration. The most obvious expressions at that time had been the difficulty to pass water, to swallow and to control the muscles in her legs. The imminent probability of change to her other bodily functions were to be expected.

From inception, the life expectation for MSA sufferers was a maximum of nine years. At this time, Sue was most likely two to four years along that time line. Facing these prospects together was absolutely the hardest and then sharing it with our four children. For us, the whole journey we'd been on through life together took on a whole new perspective, with previously unthinkable extremes of emotion.

The full impact didn't really hit me at that stage. With the home care during the day, Monday to Friday, I was able to continue work as before. Two years passed, then three, with Sue's rate of deterioration increasing dramatically as the months progressed.

Chapter 35

A New Church in Carlisle

For those first few years living in Carlisle we'd joined a church in its infancy. It had started with a few families meeting in homes and, just before we had moved in, had begun to meet in a community centre, just around the corner from our temporary accommodation. Over the previous few years it had grown significantly and changed dramatically. Some of the wonderful folk there were such a significant support for Sue, in so many different ways. However, as time passed, it seemed that something was now stalling in the church. There were lots of lovely people, mature Christians and many were part of Operation Mobilisation based in Carlisle, which included its world organisational centre for the OM ships. The leadership in the church had been changing and I was struggling with the feeling that I was not fitting in.

One day I finally came to grips with what was really happening with me. In a moment of abandon, while out for a walk in the local park with a good friend in the church, I shared my realisation. For the first time in my life I was feeling profoundly depressed. What had been enthusiasm and a passion for 'church' within me for years past, had given way to despair. I felt a hopelessness and that I had reached the end of the road.

'Is all this what you've brought us to Carlisle for, God?' was what I was verbalising. It was not just because of all that Sue was going through; 'Church in Carlisle and the whole of Cumbria seemed worse even than Cornwall and that's saying something!' My friend was very gracious and didn't try to sort me out - very wisely. It was so good for me to be letting it out to someone I felt I could trust.

Fascinating Timing

Later that week something came to mind. Somehow, I'd heard mention of a couple who had recently moved to Carlisle to start a New Frontiers church in the city. Sue and I had come to know a fair bit about the development of New Frontiers over the years. 'Why don't I drop in and meet this couple and check them out? Nothing could be lost - at the least it would be interesting.' Someone in my office, with connections, knew of this couple and got their 'phone number for me. I made the 'phone call and they agreed to me dropping by the next Sunday afternoon. The door was answered by the lady; her husband Eric was in the conservatory. She showed me through and excused herself to continue the ironing in the kitchen. That was Alison and I stepped through to meet Eric. It was a fascinating tipping point! Eric received me so warmly and naturally. He was a Scot - that was a big plus!

The backgrounds of both Eric and Alison were fascinating. Separately, they had both dramatically come to know Jesus, just a few years earlier, in the south of England where they were both working for IBM. A truly amazing transformation had taken place in their lives. They had both been living totally godless lives.

Alison was the first one; through her counsellor she had a life-changing encounter with Jesus, to the horror of partner Eric. Following her conversion, Alison just had to live with his disdain.

Some months later, under duress, Eric agreed to keep his lady sweet by sitting through an Easter Sunday service in the Anglican Church which she was attending. While standing during the service and planning his first drink when he got home, Eric was gazing at the stained-glass window at the front of the church with its representation of Jesus on the cross. He heard a voice in his head, 'I did this for you Eric!' He crumpled in the pew. At the end of the service, the vicar, who was also the counsellor who had led Alison to know Jesus, spoke with him. He then lead Eric in a prayer of confession and Eric handed his whole life over to Jesus for a brand new start. Wonderfully, it happened, big time.

Both having said goodbye to IBM, they spent some months of full-time training in a New Frontiers church. During that time, they had experienced a powerful and very specific call of God to plant a new church in Carlisle and now here they were.

It was then my turn. I shared a little about myself and what had brought Sue and I to Carlisle and now the watershed that Sue and I both felt we'd come to in the church we were attending. The afternoon disappeared. I had genuinely come alive. On the way out, I was introduced to Alison in the other room - it turned out that the door had been open and she'd listened to all that had been going on in the conservatory. In the days that followed, Sue and I together met up regularly with Eric and Alison. A new and exciting journey had definitely started.

For the past year, since they had come to Carlisle, Eric and Alison had been involved in the New Frontiers church in Keswick, about a 40 minute drive south, while they had been waiting for things to come together in Carlisle. They now wanted to introduce me to Derek who led the church in Keswick and was also supporting the other NFI churches in Cumbria.

I had no idea how Derek would receive me. I was definitely apprehensive as Eric drove us both towards Keswick that evening. To my surprise, Derek asked all about me. He listened and asked questions about my past and present. The vision for Carlisle that I was now sharing with Eric and Alison had a good airing. Derek's response was amazingly cordial, encouraging and releasing. The drive back to Carlisle with Eric was great! The next hurdle was for Sue and I, along with our daughter Beth, to say goodbye to the church we'd been attending in Carlisle. On the Sunday Sue and I stood before the church and we explained our intention and said our farewells. They graciously prayed for us and bade us farewell.

The next step was now to see what God had for us with Eric and Alison. We had a wonderful feeling of freedom and growing faith for what God had for us, as we looked to see a New Frontiers church established in this city with so much need.

Chapter 36

Sue's New Year's Day Fall

What better way to start!

About twelve months before Sue and I had met them, Eric and Alison, had been waiting for the right time to make a start in Carlisle. Following their year of training in church planting, they had been sent north from the Leicester church. For some nine months they had been a part of the Keswick New Frontiers church. What struck both Sue and I, was how personable and caring they both were. As to church, we felt we were on the same page with them and in total agreement as to the type of church we desired to be a part of. The New Frontiers model at that time seemed to be so good. What we'd seen of the way that Derek and his wife Linda, had started and continued to grow the church in Keswick was a really great model. So off we went!

Christmas Day and Boxing Day had passed. It was now New Years day and Sue encouraged me to go out to the hills for some fresh air on my own as she didn't feel up to the car ride; both our girls were away for the day with friends. Christmas Day had been quite demanding so I agreed to get out to walk in the Lake District. I don't remember what the weather was like or exactly where I went, however I got back home at about four o'clock. I put the key in the front door but it wouldn't open properly - something was stopping it. I pushed my head round the door to see what the obstacle was. I

was horrified. Sue was lying on the mat and the cold floor tiles between the closed inner door and front door, looking up at me. I squeezed in; she couldn't move. I carried her into the lounge and propped her up in a chair.

'Whatever has happened; how long have you been there?'

'Just after lunch someone rang the front door bell,' she struggled to say. 'I got to the door, but before I could open it, I must have passed out. When I came to, I found I couldn't move and my voice was so weak I couldn't even cry out. I don't know how long it's been, but I'm very cold.'

She must have lain there for at least four hours. I dialled 999. The ambulance arrived promptly and whisked her off to A&E at the Cumberland Infirmary. Vital signs were ok but she still could not move. I told them that Sue had Multiple System Atrophy. Through that evening I waited with her and eventually she was transferred as an in-patient to one of the wards. By the end of the week Sue was feeling stronger in herself, though totally unable to use her legs, let alone get out of the bed herself. It was looking as if she was not going anywhere any time soon and it turned out to be a very long stay!

Visiting Sue in the afternoon, a few days later that week, the three of us, Eric, Alison and I sat around Sue's bed. It was the first 'meeting' of the new church! Such a memorable day and experience, in so many ways!

Nine Long Months

After a month or so, Sue was transferred across the landing to the Rehab ward. This was the ward for those who'd had strokes or major heart attacks and were in a similar situation to Sue. The staff were wonderful and so patient. With their variety of skills they sought to facilitate the patients to return to as normal a life as possible, building muscles that no longer worked, rebuilding self confidence, trying to use walking frames and electric wheelchairs that could travel the roads or pavements and give back some degree of independence. Sue tried one of these electric buggies on the road behind the hospital with a view to being issued one on discharge. Unfortunately, as I watched her Sue was not able to steer in a straight line; she'd really put the wind up the instructor. He came back visibly shaken, concluding that Sue's lack of co-ordination was not going to make the roads viable! Eventually, she could use a walking frame - as long as someone was walking alongside, in case she fell. With practice, fortunately, Sue was able to control an indoor electric wheelchair so then she could begin to get around the ward and the adjacent rest room.

Sue was on that Rehab ward for nine months before home care provision could be set up. There was so much to achieve: the provision of a walking frame, an electric wheelchair and most importantly, finance for the seven in the morning to eight in the evening home-care. I got to know the hospital well over those nine months with my daily visits to Sue.

Finally, the funds needed were available and the care package was in place. There was room in our smaller downstairs living room for the hospital bed with all the trimmings and, to my surprise, my single bed as well - so I could keep an eye on her through the nights. Fortunately, several years earlier I'd installed a walk-in shower unit as part of our downstairs toilet. Sue would be able to be given a shower while in her wheelchair. The two carers did a great job coping with everything that Sue needed; handling the different pipes needed for her survival, including the liquid feeding pipe and urine pipe and, of course all the variety of medications needed throughout each day. Fortunately, Sue could still use the wheelchair to get to the car outside and, on my day off, we could often escape for a trip into the Lake District or the coast close by, or attend our Sunday morning meeting.

Chapter 37

Kings Church Carlisle

Getting Started

It may just have been the four of us at Sue's hospital bed that January afternoon but, rapidly, the word went round Carlisle, somehow! The time was evidently right.

Even though Sue was not able to join with us for many months due to being 'hospital bound', a variety of families made contact wanting to know more. Sadly, they mainly seemed to be folk who had been disillusioned with other churches and, in some cases, church in general. I guess there have always been disillusioned Christians.

Eric and Alison, along with Sue and me, decided we would push the boat out and we arranged to get together on Sunday mornings, even though Sue wasn't able to be with us for what turned out to be such a long time.

There was a family with two small children that were 'well in', right from the start. Within just a few weeks others were joining with us - another couple with their two children and also an older lady. We met in the large front room of our late Victorian terraced house. We sang, read the Bible and someone shared a prepared talk. It was so informal, and everyone including the children were involved and then of course, there was the essential shared lunch together!

Needless to say, as a few weeks went by, others came and joined with us as well. One of the couples did a great job in leading us all in praise and worship. The husband was a gifted guitarist and his wife had a great voice - they went so well together. The husband, though a firm Christian, had not been able to face church for many years. Here he now was, along with his wife and two kids, really enthusiastically involved.

For those who could make it, we met up mid-week as well, sharing vision and our life together. It didn't take long for a foreseeable problem to arise! We were getting too large a group for our front room and soon there was room for no one else.

The New Frontiers model, like most other models at the time, was to rent a larger space so more people could gather. It was a no brainer. It was needful and obvious. We found a smart new
suite of buildings in part of the Secondary School just down the road, with easy access and ideal facilities for lunch together as well. Perfect.

The start in the new location coincided with Carlisle University's new academic year. On the first Sunday, three first year students sat with us as the band led, then Eric spoke, as well as he always did; there was a freshness and excitement evident in the atmosphere. Then, of course, there was the shared food afterwards. The new students, from Newcastle, Yorkshire and Ireland, were enthusiastic and, yes, were coming back next week. We were off, with plenty of space to expand.

A couple of weeks later was a very memorable Sunday for Sue, in her wheel chair, and for me as well. Our son Tim and his family were back in the UK, visiting us on furlough from their missionary lives in Mozambique. The week before, our daughter, Hannah, had graduated at her university in Liverpool and there she was, to our great surprise, sitting in the meeting next to her brother, Tim.

For her three years in Liverpool, Hannah had lived in denial of the decision she had made many years before, to live for Jesus as his disciple. She chose to follow the ways of her fellow students, wholeheartedly, as was Hannah's way.

At the end of the meeting, evidently something was happening with Hannah and brother Tim. When we all got back home that afternoon, Hannah was transformed, radiant. With Tim, she'd faced up to her lifestyle over those past three years and called on her heavenly Father, as she chose to turn away from what had been her student lifestyle, asking for forgiveness and a fresh start. A fresh start it truly was! It was so good to have the newly transformed Hannah back.

From then on, week by week, the new Sunday meeting and everything else just grew!

A Significant Discovery

I've often thought back to those exciting times over the years. Almost always, the words of the famous song of Frank Sinatra painfully resonate with me, so true on reflection, not just for this time, but for so much of my experience in church life over the decades.

> 'Mistakes, I've made a few . . . too many to . . . '
> . . . but through it all, I did it my way!'

I could only wish that, for me, it had 'only been a few,' as Frank claimed for himself. Absolutely, I don't like the punch line at the end, which was the title of the song: 'My Way.'

Sadly, I have had to face the reality that, all too often, my driver was for 'My Way', even if it may have been with good intentions. However, I've also made a very significant discovery. Potentially, the things I can learn most in my life and with the most profound effects, are when I face up to my mistakes! I think this can be true for all of us. Put it another way: 'We can learn more from our mistakes, than from our successes!' You can quote me. The reason I feel I've learnt so much in my journey, is because I've made so many mistakes during my years! I'm now really proud of my second degree in Mistake-Making! I'm still working on my Masters. The Doctorate seems a long way off.

Over the next months and years, Kings Church Carlisle, as it became known, grew by leaps and bounds. So many good people joined the church. People came to know Jesus as Saviour and Lord for the first time. Many baptisms took place in the River Eden in the summer and the heated school swimming pool come winter. From those early days, Hannah came to play a significant part in the life of the growing church, especially doing a great job in relating and building with the growing number of students.

In the Midst of Success

When I look back to our first few months of gathering as a new church, there was one particular sadness regarding one of those first families that joined with us. They had two little children; the husband played the guitar really well and his wife sang and led the worship when we were meeting in the home. A month or so after we had started meeting with the growing bunch of folk In the school suite, the husband disappeared off the scene. A few weeks later, the rest of the family left as well. Had we changed that much?

What had appealed to him in those early days, was the intimacy and relational feel of what we had started with. Sadly, it seemed to be the price we paid as the numbers grew, even though it was what we treasured highly and sought to maintain - we still had a shared meal at the end of our Sunday meeting! Eating together was something we continued to do even when the numbers rose past a hundred and we then met in the large main school hall.

Frontier Project

Nationally, New Frontiers had an excellent training course for Christians called Frontier Project, mainly with young adults. Hannah jumped at the opportunity. Based in the home church, it was a one year course, gathering at certain regional centres one day a month for teaching Bible study, outreach methods and personal development, along with times of worship together. Every quarter, for three days, there were times when all the trainees from the north region of England got together at different venues - including Centre Parks; that was a winner, they enjoyed that one especially.

For the rest of the year, the volunteers worked supporting their local church, which was also supporting them financially during that year. It did Hannah a world of good and she thrived on it all. Her subsequent investment with the Carlisle University students resulted in many following in her footsteps and, on their graduation, joining the Frontier Project themselves. After Hannah finished her

Frontier Project she worked full-time in Kings Church with the students.

Chapter 38

The Dam Breaks

At the same time as Kings Church was growing, my running the Bible Software and Video product division within STL in Carlisle was also developing. My business life involved maintaining relationships with our, now mainly American suppliers, as well as developing our homegrown products. Bringing new products to market and just keeping the wheels turning took time and energy as this whole division was down to just me and my secretary. I had to make my annual US trip for the week long massive Christian Booksellers Convention, held in different US cities, each year in the summer. There were also trips within the UK to Christian events and summer Bible Weeks. Fortunately, I was able to leave Sue in the capable care of the carers and our wonderful daughters who were now both living at home and were very responsible.

Sue's continued down-hill journey was becoming progressively tougher for her and also for the family. Having to see her deteriorating and suffering so much, demanded that the girls and I put on our brave faces in order to support and encourage in all ways we could. There was an inevitable price being paid but was well hidden away. We had to stand strong in support.

One day, while in the office, I got a message from Keith, the company CEO. He was inviting me to lunch just the two of us, at what turned out to be a very swish restaurant in a village just outside Carlisle, well known for its excellent food.

Keith was already sitting at a table and waiting for me when I arrived. 'What would you like to drink Barry?' He asked. He ordered me a sherry. Over the past five or six years I'd got to know Keith well from our Sunrise Software days in Cornwall and then our subsequent partnership with his STL business. He had been very welcoming of me when I first moved up to Carlisle, and I'd spent several evenings with him and his wife and two daughters in their home. He had always been very warm and supportive - but he was still the CEO of what was now a mega company, having acquired so many other companies in the Christian market at home and abroad.

We talked about general things, of no real consequence, as we ate our entrée. By then I was really wondering why I'd received this invitation, out of the blue. As we started our main course, Keith casually asked how Sue was getting on. I didn't know how much he knew at that time, so I set off explaining the diagnosis and how she was now coping with developing functional degeneration. As I put it all into words I felt like a cascade of water was flooding over me. I found it harder to speak and I started sobbing as I tried to explain. I apologised but could not control it. He was smiling graciously and allowed me to continue. The closeness of the people at the tables either side increased my sense of shame, but I couldn't stop the tears and the deep sobbing. I continued to try to explain it all to Keith, while continuing to apologise.

Finally, I said that I needed to stop talking and eat the roast beef in front of me so I could try to regain control.

I settled down as Keith began to speak. 'I think the way forward from here is.' He went on to explain what he thought needed to start as soon as possible. I would step back from my role in the business, so that I had more time to be at home to support Sue and, also, to be more available in working for Kings Church in Carlisle. He would support me for the next twelve months and continue paying my current salary.

I was blown away. It was not surprising that Keith knew about the growing new church in the city, as he was also a part of the Christian community in Carlisle. He'd not asked me how I was coping, evidently what he had witnessed across that lunch table had made it abundantly clear to him.

By the time we reached the car park after our meal, I was in a far better shape to talk coherently. I was overwhelmed by the generosity of his offer and didn't need any more time to consider it. I told him it would be wonderful in all ways and I accepted and thanked him most sincerely.

As I drove away from the car park, I realised that it was the first time I had connected to what I was feeling deep down. It certainly hadn't been planned. The effect on me was like a massive dam holding back a vast amount of water which had suddenly breached and an incredible flood burst through it, clearing everything in its path. Being able to express what I felt from deep within me that lunchtime, was enabling me to connect with myself. It became so liberating and necessary in the months that lay ahead, in order to support Sue in a completely different way.

I've always wondered if that outcome was a result of my emotional display, or whether it was the reason behind that lunch appointment in the first place. It didn't make any difference either way. Within a few weeks the pressures I'd been living under were only set to increase.

Eric and I were now able to have weekly day time meetings, to plan and pray about the day to day running of the church and the way forward. Most importantly, I was available for Sue so much more.

However, I still had so much more to learn about this wonderful God-given gift of emotions!

Chapter 39

Those days in the Lakes

As the days continued, Sue was so thoughtful. She insisted that when I took my day off I should get away. She was now safe in the hands of her carers.

So I did, not every week, but when I did, I drove the few miles south to the Lake District. Those times had the same effect on me in both summer and winter; they were cathartic, exhausting, always physically stretching my body and at times so painful - those blisters on the feet and muscles complaining; all definitely a profound aid to sleeping that night! In all, they were wonderful days of connection with my Maker.

Grunting up the hillsides, getting to steep areas towards the top with the loose rocks and even, sometimes, bordering on the down right dangerous. However, always guaranteed was arriving at the peak, or the flat rocky plateaued area at the top, offering me the same effect - so wonderful; awe inspiring. Looking out on the ranges of peaks all around, sitting and gazing down the green valleys with the sheep just like dots way below, slowly gazing down to the tiny groups of distant farm buildings, then the lakes with their ever changing gorgeous colours of blues, greens and browns that was the water; and of course, there were the clouds; I got to love clouds! So varied, the effects of the

light, with rain falling in the distance. Then spinning round 180 degrees towards
the west coast of Cumbria, while holding onto my cap as I faced the stiff winds, or times when, stripped down to T shirt and shorts, there was just a gentle warm breeze.

It was wonderful, sitting soaking it all in, enjoying the reward of arrival at the peak along with that essential chocolate bar. The awesome wonder of God's creation, the privilege of being able to sweat and push the body and get there. The Psalmist put it so well,

> *O LORD, our Lord, how majestic is your name in all the earth!*
> *When I look at your heavens, the work of your fingers,*
> *the moon and the stars, which you have set in place,*
> *what is man that you are mindful of him,*
> *and the son of man that you care for him?*
> (Ps 8 vv 1, 3&4)

Exhilarating! 'Thank you Father; to know your Son, Jesus, who makes all this so different. You created it all and gave us the ability to see you in it all. You have the power of creation, life and even death in your hands. What can I do but praise and thank you. I can trust you. You absolutely, have my Sue in your hands too.'

Finally returning home before the carer knocked off, I was totally exhausted, but so refreshed; the body may have needed some TLC but I was a new man inside, needing to face the week ahead with a refreshed perspective on everything.

A Wonderful Discovery
During those times I discovered 'the camera'! I'd had one

as a teenager, but now the 'digital camera' had emerged. It came with me on my day off in the hills but how to use it was a very slow discovery. Eventually the discovery was beginning to bloom. A half reasonable photo, was so much more than just 'point and click.' Here were these weekly, wonderful panoramas, gorgeous sunrises and fabulous sunsets across the lakes - and now my photographs were on the way!

What finally did it for me was joining the Carlisle Camera Club that met once a week. That was really take off for me! Rapidly, I learnt so much. Photography was opening up a whole new experience of the world. I jest not - I began to notice the world around me in ways I'd never seen before. I'd taken so much for granted, but now I was seeing the wonderful colours, the sun through the trees in different seasons and, of course, those clouds which were for ever changing the shapes and light dispersal, the wonderful shadows playing with the rays of the sun. Walking and climbing the peaks took on a whole new excitement. The camera opened up to me great opportunities into the future.

Chapter 40

Eric's Call to Leave

The years passed. So much good. So much change. Well over a hundred folk were a part of the church and the Sunday meeting was now in the main school hall of another of the Carlisle secondary schools. It worked very well for us. We had a healthy emphasis on small groups led by excellent couples who were doing a great job. The church office with its meeting area which had lots of sofas and armchairs, provided us with the opportunity of meeting up in smaller or larger groups. It was an office for the church secretary to manage things in and also a base for the former students on the Frontier Project. They were involved in the day to day life of the church and evangelism in the city, when not on their away training.

After the early beginnings, Eric and I had both been established as elders of Kings Church Carlisle by the leaders of the Cumbria New Frontiers churches, as was the way.

An annual high spot for all the northern region NF churches was the week-long summer conference, held on farm land in the north east. The first one was memorable for several reasons. The main speaker was Terry Virgo, who was so good for his solid and excellent bible teaching. One late afternoon before the evening meeting, Eric and I were taking a walk around the camping field. That walk is indelibly engraved in my memory. Eric told me that God had spoken to him that morning in the shower. The time was right. He and Alison should leave Carlisle to start a new church in Scotland. Eric was born and bred Scottish though his wife, Alison, is an Essex girl. Every fibre in my body cried out, No! No! No! I responded, 'Eric you can't leave. Please. The church is not ready for this, nor am I'. The church was only about five years on from the start! By the next day, very graciously, Eric agreed to stay. Phew!

The church continued to thrive, though, sadly, during this period some folk had come for a while and then moved on it happens. There were certainly many challenges and disappointments, but also so much good was happening all around us. God had poured out his wonderful unmerited grace and mercy, for which we were very thankful.

Chapter 41

It happened so suddenly!

A few years passed, life went on and Sue progressively changed. The most heart rending effect for me was feeling that I was losing my Sue! As her face muscles stopped responding, we all lost that wonderful, endearing smile that was Sue. Of course she tried to smile, but it was cruel. Whether she ever knew the transformation or not, I never knew, but I was certainly not going to draw attention to it.

The time came when nights were getting difficult. Sue, in distress, would wake me in the small hours. 'There's someone at the window.' The curtains were drawn closed. I got up and parted the curtains but saw no one. I reassured Sue that there was no one there, trying to put her mind to rest and get her back to sleep.

Our house was part of the standard Victorian terraces in that area, built back in the 1880s. Outside, the small back yard was surrounded by an eight foot high brick wall incorporating a small garage backing onto the lane running behind our yard. Hence, all the back yards along our row were quite secure, added to which, there was a street light directly behind our ground floor bedroom, that even shone through our curtained window. As the weeks passed, unfortunately, the occurrences became more frequent and Sue's evident fear was increasing. 'There's a man crawling along the top of the wall outside, I can see his face!'

It was becoming harder and harder to reassure her that there was no one there and we were safe. Her distress level and sleeplessness was now extreme. At a regular visit to Sue's designated GP I mentioned it. She agreed they needed to look into it. The doctor arranged for a spell of respite care for Sue at the local Hospice Care Home. Sue had spent a week there a few years before so that I would be able to have a week away. She had loved the care and friendliness at the hospice, so it was arranged.

At the very last minute, it was cancelled. The hospice told me they could not have anyone who was hallucinating. Understandable, but so sad. A few weeks later, new arrangements were made for Sue to spend a week or so in the local hospital instead, in order that tests could be carried out.

Hospital

The preparations were made for Sue to go into the hospital on a Friday. I drove her there with some bed clothes and a carrier bag containing enough of her meds and the small containers of liquid feed to last for the duration of her short stay.

On entering the ward we were greeted by a lady care assistant so I wheeled Sue into the single room in order to get her into the waiting bed. I was quite taken aback when she told me to wait outside, while she got Sue into the bed. I replied that as I was her husband and primary carer, I should do it. She insisted. I stood in the corridor and she closed the door.

Five minutes later the door opened again and I was let in. Sue was smiling, sitting up in the bed. The care assistant said she'd be back later. As she left she mentioned that Sue had said that she was thirsty, so she had given Sue a drink through the straw in one of the small food containers that I'd left in the carrier bag before leaving the room. I was totally shocked at what she told me - there was nothing I could do.

I stayed and chatted with Sue for a while and later took my leave, assuring her that I'd back to visit the next day. The next day she was on a main ward of eight patients and as it was now Saturday, there wouldn't be any tests until Monday.

That Saturday evening I got a 'phone call from the Ward Sister. Sue was not well and they were running some tests. Early on Sunday morning I went in to see her again. The Sister caught me on the way in. Sue had developed pneumonia. She was on a high dose of antibiotics; she did not look well. I knew exactly what was happening. For some years, the only way Sue could be fed was with those liquid feeds, through a pipe straight into her stomach. As she could no longer swallow, anything taken by mouth would go straight into her lungs.

When I got home I called her mother and brother, who lived in North Wales and they said they would come right up.

That Sunday evening Sue had deteriorated profoundly; she was conscious but very weak. Our daughters Hannah and Beth were with me, then Sue's mother and brother arrived. Sue was dying. Our son Marc could not make it up from Cornwall in time, neither could Tim who, with his family, was living and working in Mozambique. Late that night we said our final farewells and Sue died. The Ward Sister gave me Sue's wedding ring and watch as I left.

A week later the funeral took place. The support from family, friends and church friends was amazing. It was so good that Tim had made the trip back from Africa in time and Marc was with us from Cornwall. I had requested that the service should be one of celebration and it really was-celebrating Sue's special life and the certainty she had carried to the end. She was now in the perfect presence of her loving heavenly Father.

The songs reflected the atmosphere of the whole event, led by our friend Eric: Celebration, but also such sadness and loss. For Sue, above all, release from so many months and years of progressive disintegration.

Chapter 42

Away from it All

After the funeral Eric and Alison encouraged me to take some time away, for a complete change. It was the right decision. I needed time out following the build up over the previous months and years. It was coming to the end of March and I had the bright idea it had to be Cornwall.

I booked a bed and breakfast on the Lizard peninsular in west Cornwall for a week. The weather was spectacular for March.

It turned out to be a very special time, not just because it was spring in Cornwall, with fabulous weather, but the opportunity of dropping in on two couples who had played a very special part in our lives at different times over past years.

The nights were cold, but glorious days of windless sunshine. As an extra bonus, there were hardly any tourists around - except for me, I suppose! What to do with the freedom? I felt there was so much that I had to cope with.

I could not help but think about how it had all developed so quickly, when Sue only went to the hospital for those tests. If only the care assistant had not been so foolish and had allowed me into the room as Sue's principle carer! With hind sight it was all so unnecessary. Sue would still be alive. No way would I have let her drink any liquid that would kill her. It was so hard to deal with what had happened, but I had to come to terms with it all. It had happened so fast, in a matter of four days.

That week on the Lizard in Cornwall surpassed my wildest expectations. The glorious sunshine across the vast seas and the gentle breezes, in March! The physicality of that long walk from Helston back down to the B&B at the Lizard village; those seemingly countless steep descents down to so many coves, and then of course, the steep hauls up again to the cliff path. Wonderfully, with so few people around, it made it even better; I could shout, yell and sing out to my Heavenly Father without offending anybody!

I finally reached the B&B, having walked my twelve miles, just in time for the evening meal, totally exhausted, but at peace. The following Bible passages had been coming alive for me:

'For as the heavens are higher than the earth,
so are my ways higher than your ways
and my thoughts than your thoughts'.
Psalm 103:11

'For I am sure that neither death nor life, nor angels nor rulers,
nor things present nor things to come, nor powers, nor height nor depth,
nor anything else in all creation,
will be able to separate us from the love of God in Christ Jesus our
Lord.'
Paul in Romans 8:38-39

And above all Paul's declaration,

'we know that for those who love God all things work together for good,
for those who are called according to his purpose' Romans 8:28

Jesus Culture have a great song, quoting from Psalm 30 verse 5, the refrain has the words:

'Your love never fails,
There may be pain in the night -
but joy comes in the morning.'

    I sang this song repeatedly along those cliff tops, with growing conviction and a wonderful sense of release. 'Yes, I believe it's true. My Sue is in your hands. Finally, release for a good and faithful servant. But, I will really miss her.'

Chapter 43

Death. What's it really about?

Beware! The 'Big D' word!

All too often in our culture today the Big 'D' word has been relegated to the unseemly and is avoided at all costs. 'Death.' Instead, it's referred to as 'passing away' or 'passing on' or, maybe, being 'in a better place.' During my life time certain words and language have gone out of favour to be replaced by alternatives that won't offend anyone. Words and phrases that cause discomfort in us, anxiety, or even genuine naked dread, are replaced with words that might bring a little reassurance.

A prime example of this, the word is 'd-e-a-t-h;' the 'Big D', and everything to do with dying. Such words confront us with our mortality, like it or not. They speak of something which is utterly out of our control. However, sooner or later it will confront each of us with a finality which we cannot reason or argue with.

It's surprising, however, when pushed, that the vast majority of folk calling themselves atheists or, more commonly, agnostics, when a loved one dies use language that implies there is something, somewhere, after physical death. We humans can't bear to think that our loved ones have now become just smoke in the crematorium. If so, what does this say about us when our time on this earth is up? Is the very best that's on offer just 'wishful thinking?'

So Sadly Missed

Missed, or so often, totally ignored, is the profoundly credible evidence of so many first hand witnesses to the resurrection of Jesus. Three days and nights after very publicly dying, then over a period of weeks, being seen by many people, actually walking, talking and eating! Such evidence in our judicial system would be incontrovertible 'evidence to convict!'

As if the objective evidence was not enough, the up to date clincher has to be the experience of many thousands of people down through the centuries. So many who, when challenge and conflict came, were willing to give up their lives, rather than deny their experience of this personal living Jesus.

When push comes to shove, it's not conviction of religious belief that counts. Adhering to a 'religion' may make us feel good but can only take us just so far. When we individually experience a personal transformation, a peace, a joy, a sense of completion, like nothing we have ever experienced before, our attention is captivated with a conviction that is so much more than a theory or wishful thinking. The Holy Spirit, God himself, does his job! Amazingly, he really does make Jesus real to those who start and continue the journey with him.

Looking Back

As a youngster visiting my grandparents, when the conversation with my mother turned to news of a relation having just died, I couldn't miss the softened, pained tones, the Scottish 'oh no' and the awareness of the dark cloud settling over the room. Understandable to a degree, my grandfather had experienced the trenches of the First World War, having lost half of his intestines and only just having survived, with severe shell shock, plus the horrors of seeing so many of his close friends killed in front of him.Then he with his wife and teenage daughter had to endure living in South London through the blitz of the Second World War. I was affected profoundly by my grandparents, but I held it all in. Death was off limits!

My father, in his early twenties, survived the D Day Normandy landings on day two. Along with many thousands, he survived the cruel months of the horrendous experience of the Falaise Gap in northern France, when allied troops were trapped for three months under constant German shelling. So many never returned home- something never spoken of in my home until much later in my life. Had Post Traumatic Stress Disorder been identified back then, both my father and grandfather would definitely have been among the many!

Despite my father's breakdown some years later, my parents came through those shaping experiences. They both shared a life changing conviction, a certainty and a sense of a positive future. Both mum and dad, in their mid teens and, independently of each other, had made a life and death changing discovery of the resurrected, living, Jesus. Sadly, they were the only ones in both their families to make that discovery.

A generation later, when Sue was forty six, she was given that sentence of death at the local hospital. We'd sat there together, across the desk from the two doctors who gave the diagnosis - it was just a matter of time progressive deterioration, but the result of Parkinson's Disease was inevitable.

That day is also indelibly printed upon all of my senses. We kept it from our two children who were still at home at that time. We closed the door of our room and Sue and I wept together. Family life as we'd known it was coming to an end, progressively, but terminally. Little did we both know and little did we really understand that day of the big one - 'death'.

A little later, when we felt we could cope, we shared it with all four of our children. It was so hard. The youngest of our girls, Beth, was not yet in her teens, with Hannah just five years older. One of the boys had left home and one was at University. I can't think what it would have been like without the certain conviction that death was not going to be the end for their mum. Death is just the beginning for all who accept this free gift of new life that Jesus has paid for - those who choose to make him the boss of their lives. This is a million miles from accepting or acknowledging a religious system, nor is it wishful thinking. This indeed is Good News. Thank you heavenly Father that my Sue died with this certainty.

Where We're At

If there was ever a time in my whole life when our society had a crying need for the truth and genuine reality of a hope in the 'after life', it's now.

We've made so much progress in so many areas of our culture. Despite so many limitations, the opportunities of longer life expectancy, significant growth in health and well being, opportunities for education and individual advancement are being experienced across the board.

Discoveries in so many wonderful areas of life are believed to have removed the need for any Creator and obviously there is deemed to be so much evidence pointing to the full stop of death. 'Religion', of course, is no longer required, in fact it is positively destructive and a laughable, out of date, crutch - as the 'Death of God' movement heralded in the middle years of the last century.

The Apostle Paul writes his first letter to the church in Corinth that he knows so well. He was the one who had been the first to introduce the people there to the good news of Jesus. So many of the Corinthians had responded and, since then, many more had been added. Sadly, Paul had come to hear that, in his absence, false ideas and wrong practices had developed. He writes to correct and emphasise the importance of vital areas of belief, as well as behaviour. The whole letter is profoundly relevant for us today.

As Paul gets to the end of his letter, in chapter 15, he confronts many of the doubts of the Corinthians which are exactly the same for us today. The very foundation of the Christian faith; what sets it apart from all other religions and faith systems, *'For I delivered to you as of first importance what I also received: that Christ died for our sins in accordance with the scriptures, that he was buried, that he was raised on the third day in accordance with the Scriptures, and that he appeared to Cephas, then to the twelve.'* (1 Cor 15:3-4) Paul then applies the vital importance of the veracity, of Jesus being alive after he was witnessed as dead and buried, to the future experience of each of us who put our trust in him. Death is not the end. Jesus demonstrates and proves it! *'But in fact Christ has been raised from the dead, the first fruits of those who have fallen asleep.'* (1 Cor 15:20). Not stopping there, Paul goes on to explain the transformation of our physical bodies when we die. As sure as Jesus rose from the dead, *'When the perishable puts on the imperishable, and the mortal puts on immortality, then shall come to pass the saying that is written: Death is swallowed up in victory.'* (1 Cor 15:54).

This indeed is victory! For those who have received what Jesus offers us on this earth, death, the 'Big D' word no longer holds fear. Death is our ultimate freedom: knowing Him, as He has always known us.

Chapter 44

Faith

What really is 'faith'? Language and use of language is a fascinating tool; it's our primary means of communication, forever changing and developing. Words that once meant one thing, gradually change to mean something different - sometimes profoundly different! 'Hope' is a prime example of this. It's a commonly used word. The word hope, all too often, is now used and understood to be 'wishful thinking'.

The term 'the faith' is used as the blanket term for the tenets of a religious system. It's the way we refer to the distinctives of the many religious systems the Buddhist faith, the Hindu faith, the Christian faith or indeed the Atheist faith. They all bring their individual world views.

Paul does a great job as he unwraps the results of 'faith' in Jesus in chapters 4 and 5 of his letter to the Romans. This 'faith' has absolutely nothing to do with 'wishful thinking'!

Paul uses the life of Abraham in the Old Testament to explain faith by its consequences. Abraham received what God had spoken to him and lived accordingly, despite all the obstacles and challenges that seemed to make God's promises utterly impossible and even ridiculous. In a nutshell Paul uses these words, referring to Abraham, *'No distrust made him waver concerning the promise of God, but he grew strong in his faith as he gave glory to God, fully convinced that God was able to do what he had promised. That is why his faith was counted to him as righteousness.'* (Romans 4 vv 21-22).

Paul uses the word 'counted' in this chapter six times. The Greek word here is used in two ways. Firstly it refers to a numerical calculation, for example, certain numbers make a fixed result: 2 plus 4 always equals 6. The second way the same word is used is metaphorically, referring to actions which are counted, reckoned, or considered definitely to be the result - an absolute certainty in the future.

Abraham took what God had said to him and lived as if it was a done deal, despite the seeming stupidity of it! That is what this faith thing is about it's up to God to make it happen.

Paul continues in verses 23 and 24, *'The words, it was counted to him were not written for his sake alone, but ours also. It will be counted to us who believe in him who raised from the dead Jesus our Lord.'* Just so for you and me. The consequences of our faith in Jesus, who he is and what he has done for us, are in Father God's hands.

The Apostle James, believed to be one of the brothers of Jesus, saw and experienced so much of the life, actions, death and resurrection of his brother Jesus. James understood the vital importance of faith in action. In the second verse of chapter two of James' letter to the churches across the then known Christian world, he sums up what he has been writing previously, in verses 14 to 25, with the blunt statement, *'Faith apart from works is dead.'* This is the faith that demands we make the choice to trust our Heavenly Father and act on that choice not just think about it. So, getting down to the nitty gritty, what is, or, better still, how do we exercise faith in practical living? Easy? Never! It's been such a long, slow journey for me. Slowly, I'm beginning to discover bit by bit, every day walking with Jesus, that there is absolutely nothing I can get right without his enabling, through dependance on his provision of his Holy Spirit. Here are several elements of faith in practice that I'm discovering. Please do read on a significant element of faith is trusting.

Chapter 45

Trust

The Man of Action Steps Up

The disciples see Jesus walking towards them, on the crest of the waves! Peter stands and shouts to Jesus, *'Lord, if it is you, command me to come to you on the water.'* (v28). Jesus replies, 'Come.' Peter jumps out of the boat, eyes fixed on Jesus and walks toward him, also on the top of the roaring waves. Wow! In the light of all that they'd witnessed that previous day, yes, Peter was full of faith. He hears the call of Jesus and puts his trust in what he knows and has seen Jesus doing. In a flash he makes the choice and puts it into action. Peter too is walking on the vicious water! But then verse 30 comes, *'When he saw the wind, he was afraid, and beginning to sink he cried out, Lord, save me.'* Jesus immediately reached out his hand and took hold of him. Peter, you were doing so well! You were doing all the right things, you started so well. Your trust was one hundred per cent in Jesus, you'd seen it so much through the months and so recently, what he did with that food yesterday. This Jesus is so trustworthy! But what went so wrong? He took his eyes off Jesus and the doubt took over. *'O you of little faith, why did you doubt?'* (v 31) We can hear the sadness in Jesus' words as he stretches out his hand and brings Peter back onto the boat with him.

This part of Peter, sadly, I can relate to so well, maybe we all can, it seems to be an integral part of our human condition. But Peter did get two things right! Peter demonstrated two cardinal aspects of Faith, they are making the choice and acting on it.

Jesus Teaches Trust

It was an absolutely amazing experience for those first disciples of Jesus. About 5,000 men, women and children, had followed Jesus to a remote area on the banks of the Sea of Galilee. They'd seen him do wonderful miracles of healing and they wanted to see more and maybe experience them for themselves. Jesus spends the rest of that day telling His massive audience the Good News He was heralding. Now it was late in the day, everyone was hungry and there were no shops for many miles! Jesus asks his disciples to find out how much food the people had. The result was five loaves and two fish. A laughable amount! He tells his disciples to ask the crowd to all sit down; He takes the bread and fish, breaks it and the disciples pass it around to all the hungry people. They all eat until they are stuffed! The disciples see it happen, before their very eyes and doubtless tasted it as well. Wow!

As the day ends, Jesus goes off on his own, up the hillside, to be with his Father. Some hours later the disciples are in their boat in the middle of the sea of Galilee, heading back home. For several of the disciples, as fishermen, those waters were home territory; man and boy they'd lived through the local stories and even had personal experience of how volatile the lake could be. Out of the blue, a fierce dark wind could drive through the lake turning it into a death trap.

Oh, no! Now it's happening to them. They had very good cause to be petrified for their lives; quite possibly they were now going to be driven by the force of the gale onto rocks, or the massive overwhelming waves that could destroy them any moment. Then they see Jesus coming to them through the dark - he's walking on the waves! The disciples think they're seeing a ghost! But Jesus immediately spoke to them saying, *'Take heart; it is I. Do not be afraid.'* (Matthew 14:27ff).

What an amazing twenty four hours those disciples experienced. Five thousand people, including themselves, fed with a days worth of food out of a few fish and loaves. Once again, Jesus demonstrates that there is something very special at work here, through Him. Then, to crown it all, later in the day Jesus appears and demonstrates that He can even intervene in an acute life or death situation; their own life or death.

Chapter 46

Oil & Water - Introverts & Extroverts

There was someone in Kings Church Carlisle who was puzzling me. Colin and Rachel, his wife, with their two young sons, were well engaged with the church and were currently long term missionaries with Operation Mobilisation's ships ministry. They were now working from the world HQ in Carlisle.

The months had passed and I felt I ought to try and get to know Colin better; I knew he was good value. I suggested we get together some evening and have a chat. Deal. We decided to meet up one Tuesday evening at a nice pub on the outskirts of Carlisle. It was a great setting, a summer's evening and we sat on one of the picnic type tables with fitted benches, at the back of the pub.

While we slowly supped our pints we talked about Colin and Rachel's past life, of the many years visiting countless ports around the world, as part of the OM Ships Ministry. It was truly fascinating to hear what those ten years had been like for them both. Colin's speciality was IT. Eventually they had been transferred to the OM home office in Germany and spent the following years overseeing the IT structure for the OM ships around the world. Colin made many trips to the different ships across the globe to develop and fix their vital IT systems. During those years in Germany both their two young boys had been born.

Colin continued their fascinating story; for the last couple of years, as a family, they'd been in Carlisle where the global OM HQ had been re-located. Their life's journey had been full of so many challenges and wonderful experiences, in so many countries.

It was a great evening and was now getting pretty dark and a tad chilly. We both agreed it had been a good time together and said we would meet up again at the same place, a fortnight later.

Two weeks later, at the same time we were sitting with a pint each. Colin wanted to hear about Kings Church, how it had started and where I thought it was going.

As the evening went on something really struck me. I had been talking on a variety of subjects and noticed that he was looking towards me with a very pensive face. I asked for his take on what I had been saying. He continued to look at me, and said nothing. How strange. 'You must have some thoughts on all this Colin,' I said. He made no reply but just nodded his head slowly, smiling at me. I asked again for a response but he just continued nodding with a knowing smile. I must confess I was totally lost. Was he completely opposed to all that I'd been saying, but was too polite to disagree, or what?

The time had gone, there was work for both of us the next day, so we agreed to meet again in another two weeks. We parted and Colin thanked me for our meeting. I drove home totally mystified.

The Months Passed

We continued to get together regularly and soon it was well into the autumn, which made a significant change our time was now spent next to the roaring fire in the pub lounge. We were definitely getting to know each other better and, for me, our evenings together with that one pint of lager, were not to be missed. Nevertheless, I still didn't understand the way Colin was responding in our growing relationship. 'Was it me, or was it Colin?'

One of those evenings particularly sticks in my memory. Colin's wife, Rachel, had to be out that particular night, so we arranged that the two of us would meet at their home, to be there for the kids.

I was taken completely by surprise that evening. Colin mentioned that he had just passed his final exam as an aeroplane pilot! What? I thought he was pulling my leg. No, he was very serious. He'd worked his way up over past years through the different levels, in order to gain the certificates needed and now he was qualified to take the responsibility of chief pilot.

'Come, I'll show you' he said, as he sat at his desktop computer in the lounge. 'Earlier today I flew from England to this airport in Germany.' He pointed at the screen. The route he'd taken was marked with speed, winds and all sorts of other information, on the aerial map representing the descent and safe landing, with a voice from the airport tower in the background, which had been giving him vital landing instructions.

Colin was grinning at me as the penny was dropping for me; he was flying virtual flights. I was then experiencing, for the first time, amazing passion and enthusiasm from my friend Colin. It all sounded out of this world; everything Colin was explaining to me had taken place in real time. Actual people, somewhere in the world had been fulfilling the identical roles and functions of all the professional roles necessary in order to fly planes round the globe. It was totally incredulous, could this really be true? Colin explained more, very patiently. He had built up exactly the same number of air miles and experience necessary to qualify for any commercial airline pilot. Now Colin was a Flight Captain!

The rest of the evening, with coffee not lager, was a complete revelation for me. He explained more of the detail and the years it had taken him to get this far. I was experiencing the consummate passion and the expression of such enthusiasm from Colin. This was a totally different Colin!

A Revelation

The next occasion we met I expressed my journey of confusion. 'So often, Colin, when we meet, you seem to just sit there saying nothing or, when you do, you seem so reserved. The other week when we met, I experienced so much enthusiasm and passion from you about your flying. I don't get it. Help me out Colin, I know you're also enthusiastic about Jesus, mission and church.'

He responded quickly, 'Well, I'm not like you. I can't give a quick response when I don't have one. I'm processing what you're saying; it can take quite a long time. I'm an internal processor, an introvert.'

The rest of that evening disappeared as he explained it so well. 'When I'm faced with something that is new to me, or needs a considered response, it's a slow process. In my head I see maybe a thousand and one different options. I have to visit each one and weigh it, reason it through and see if it carries weight. Even if one does, I have to go through all the others and make sure that there isn't a better response. As I guess you've seen, Barry, the more important the subject is for me, the longer it can take to arrive at a response that I'm happy and convinced with.'

I sat processing what he was telling me. Yes, I could see it. I'd never heard all this before. It was a revelation and the clarity and enthusiasm with which my friend was explaining it all made complete sense.

Colin continued, 'I'm an introvert, and maybe, more so than many introverts. I have to process everything in detail, before I make a response, it's the way I am, it's me.' He went on. 'I understand that you, Barry, are so different to me and it's so good to be able to share all this with you. I tend to think that, maybe, you're more of an extrovert?'

Colin had hit the nail on the head. I'd never really thought into the area before but now what he was saying about himself in contrast to me, was making complete sense; I am definitely more of an external processor; I guess I am a bit of an extrovert!

We parted that evening and I had so much to think about and work through. How valuable it was with regard to Colin, but now I began to see, and understand how I could relate it to people in the future.

A while later Colin mentioned a book that he'd found so encouraging and helpful. I didn't waste any time in obtaining a copy. It was the experience of an American church pastor who was also definitely an internal processor. He recounts the painful journey he had to make in church relationships, when he'd felt so 'odd' and out of place in an extrovert world. He tells how he'd also come through and learned so many wonderful lessons.

I thoroughly recommend it to you if you too want to learn more: 'Introverts in the Church' (Finding our place in an extroverted culture) by Adam S. McHugh. IVP Books 2009.

Chapter 47

Final Notice to Leave

Exactly one year after the bombshell Eric had dropped at the first Family Conference, we were now at the second Family Conference at the end of July. Eric and I went for a walk round the site again. The previous year at the Conference, Eric had heard an audible voice while in the shower. Today God had spoken to him again; he and Alison were both in agreement. Now was the time for them to move north to Scotland with a view to church plant in a new area. This time they were absolutely convinced of the rightness; it was just a matter of when. A month later, in September, they were making ready for the off.

I willingly helped Alison and Eric move their belongings and to drive some of their furniture in the hired van up to Glasgow. It was so good being able to serve them and see them into their new rented apartment and it was the very least I could do, to bid them farewell, but it felt so hard continuing without them both

Their leaving was definitely a mixed blessing. They would be enormously missed by me for absolute certain. Very graciously, they offered the use of their house to my recently married daughter, Hannah and husband, Dan. Now their house was just two doors down from where I lived. How good that was: They'd spent their first year of marriage in Carlisle, ten minutes walk away - now they would be even closer. I felt so spoilt.

Dan was working at Centre Parks in a nearby town and Hannah, having learnt much in a previous year with the New Frontiers one year training programme, was well away, overseeing and encouraging the two uni graduates who were also doing the Frontier Project training year. The three of them did a fantastic job with the many students who were becoming a part of the church. Dan and Hannah were also leading a great home group.

There was so much encouragement in the whole life of the church in the years that followed, as it continued to grow and develop. New people were joining us; there were times when the Sunday meetings were exceptionally good. The Saturday night barn dances we held were very memorable and a great opportunity to engage with non-church friends; they were great fun, though always totally exhausting!

Thinking back to those years, though hard work and very demanding, I had a real sense of fulfilment, in a whole new way. In many ways I was realising that what I was now doing 'was me'. That was a very significant discovery; however, that's not to say that I did it well!

The time came and Tim, one of our church members, was brought into eldership. After being on my own for a few years, I was thankful that it was now going to be two of us in eldership.

Chapter 48

Joy and Heartache

It was so special getting to know people in and through the church over those years; to be able to share life with folk from so many backgrounds, nationalities and on such different journeys.

During those Carlisle years there was much joy, weddings, babies born and relationships started that have stood the test of time. God was doing amazing things in rebuilding families, fun, laughter and so much to rejoice in and thank our heavenly Father for. Those Barn Dances and other outreach events, with people coming to know Jesus and lots of baptisms; the very special Christmas events we held in a city centre hotel ballroom and so much more. It was so good to be living in such a mixed community. There were folk in good jobs with regular incomes, but also many still living with the legacy of 'working class' Carlisle, but with much of the traditional industry long gone.

Poverty for many was a reality. The price paid stretched family relationships. Escape into addictions were always costly and destructive. I learnt so much, indeed, it was such a privilege to be confided in and to have the opportunity of trying to play a part in making a difference when there was so much pain. Jesus experienced pain and so much heartbreak. Wonderfully, the living Jesus can and did make a difference. Hope and change did happen. Don't we all have issues to deal with?

I learnt so much about myself and who I was during those years. I'm also certain that I learnt most through the painful times.

Sanju & Emily

Sanju and Emily were such a good couple; they hadn't been married for very long. We'd known Emily through her university days and her husband, originally from Nepal, had been with us for a while before they were married.

They were exciting days and they were now expecting their first child. As always they had many months to wait through the progressive changes taking place, but with all the exciting anticipation. The day finally came for the delivery, but there were complications. It had to be a hospital delivery, the newborn had serious heart defects, but she was alive. Mother, daughter and dad were immediately transferred to Intensive Care at the Royal Victoria Infirmary in Newcastle. It was a terrible shock for mum and dad. Surgery was going to be needed.

A long ordeal began. Multiple operations were required with the baby in the intensive care baby unit and a special room close by for mum and dad to spend the nights. They both had to be there to look after their baby girl and also just in case something happened. It was a very long and tumultuous nine months for this special young couple. As a church we prayed for them. Their close friends visited, as I also did on numerous occasions.

There were four bays in this specialist unit. The staff were very special, they had to be in order to face not just the physical and technical demands, but most telling, to face their own personal emotional challenges, but, of course, it was hardest for mum and dad. The staff were amazingly caring, patient and flexible professionals. They carried out so many surgical operations endeavouring to modify the partially developed heart.

The procedures held the prospect of finally fixing the issues with very high hopes. After nine months of so much loving care and surgery, their baby died. It was an overwhelming sadness for all involved. I counted it a great privilege to be asked to take the funeral and burial back in Carlisle.

I know that, in the midst of the unspeakable grief that mum and dad were gallantly seeking to bear, they were able to receive deep comfort from the assurance of our loving heavenly Father's care especially for this little one. Sanju and Emily's strong personal faith in Jesus made all the difference for them both as they faced the days that followed. Emily's mother was a nominal Christian; I could see her assenting to it all, but it was so sad to see her grappling with the right words, but without the assurance they could bring. The baby's grandad? He was a man! He didn't show anything, but was clearly struggling to try and comfort his wife the grandmother who had just lost her first grandchild. I did my best on that desperately painful day. I was invited to the gathering of the immediate family after the burial, but felt so useless. By the end of the time together the grandmother seemed particularly open to talking about faith in Jesus - her heart was so open. I just had to leave it all in Father's hands. That day was a profound challenge to the state of my heart.

The funeral day was not the end of the story, however for Sanju and Emily; this great couple now have two lovely children and they're still walking with Jesus.

Such a Painful Memory

Alan was in his late forties when he started coming to Kings Church. He was showing a lot of interest. He had come across Christianity in his school years, as was the case for the rest of his very 'Carlisle' family - all born and bred locals! However the reality of a living Jesus was not part of the traditional package, it was nominal Christian tradition celebrated at Christmas and Easter. Within a few months Alan had committed himself to Jesus and was significantly affected by the complete forgiveness of Jesus; and he chose also to be baptised in water. Like us all he had a past - a wife and children but, sadly, they were now in his past, so he lived on his own. I got to know Alan well over the months that followed. He was a gifted fellow, obviously an able enthusiast at fly fishing and, at that time, had been starting a business in tattooing I was fascinated as he showed me all his gadgets and equipment and showed me 'in principle' how it worked with the great variety of designs and artwork. I still wasn't tempted to give it a try - in fact quite the opposite!

It wasn't long after those early days of getting to know Alan and regularly spending time with him that he mentioned he was getting pain in his back. Within a few months the pain was beginning to restrict what he could do. The GP explained that it was muscle strain and he needed to take it gently with light exercise.

A few more months and he couldn't move off his chair. He had scans at the hospital, but they couldn't find anything untoward, suggesting that it was 'in his mind.' What could he say, what could he do but lump it and try to live with the worsening pain.

It got to a point when at least he was getting a carer coming to his single bedroom ground floor council flat twice a day to wash and feed him. Still there was no further diagnosis. I was now visiting him regularly, praying for him, getting the church to pray and doing whatever I could.

Something happened, Alan was being transferred to the Royal Victoria Infirmary in Newcastle. A couple of days later I visited him. I'd already heard the news; finally scans had revealed he had advanced cancer of the lower spine. All these years later I can still feel the overwhelming sensation I felt as I finally walked up the corridor towards the single bedroom where Alan was lying. It was in a very remote isolation area of the hospital. Why an isolation area?

There was Alan lying in the bed, as weak as a wet rag, totally wrung out, with a noble effort at a smile. He knew the diagnosis was terminal, he didn't need to be told. What a way and what a place to die. It was clinically heartless and no family had come to see him. Overwhelming. We talked of Alan's certain future with Jesus because of the decisions and actions he had taken those months before, in accepting the sacrifice that Jesus, the Son of God, had made on his behalf. Then the profound significance of the resurrection of Jesus, demonstrating that death was not the end! God the Father brought Jesus out of the grave - preparing the way for me and Alan. 'This is good news, big time, for you Alan. This room is not the end for you nor - me!'

Two days later Alan died.

To my surprise, after Alan had died his sister got in touch with me. She and her family lived a few doors down from Alan on the same estate. She obviously knew of me through Alan. She asked me if I would conduct the funeral at the crematorium. That was a surprise. Of course I had to agree, for Alan's sake. The day came and just about all the pews were packed full at the crematorium, a goodly contingent from our church were there to support, but it was mainly Alan's family; there were so many of them, brothers, sisters, uncles and aunts, plus loads of kids as well. Where did they all come from all of a sudden?

I did my level best. 'Boy, I need your help, Father!' I told the story of what I knew of Alan from the past few years; how he had accepted Jesus as his Saviour and that Alan died knowing forgiveness. I tried as best I could not to sound too 'religious' and certainly not condemning.

As people filed out in silence at the end, I stood at the door, as one should. Hands were shaken and complementary words were expressed by family members - I guessed it was the 'right' thing to do. To my great surprise I was invited to the family 'remembrance' afterwards, at the local pub. Umm. Well why ever not? I thought, and so I joined with them.

I'm so glad I did. The family was amazingly welcoming and friendly. Maybe what I had said earlier had not totally put them off? I had some wonderful conversations with some of the folk over the next few hours. These were definitely not 'church going people' but that wasn't a problem and what an opportunity it turned out to be. They had real practical questions about life, death, God and Jesus.

'Thank you Alan for this opportunity! Heavenly Father you know what you're doing with these people and the seeds sown.' I finally took my leave, everyone else was obviously set fair to see the rest of the evening out at their local.

Such heart-softening times. It seems that no matter what the situation, my gracious heavenly Father always used people, one way or another, to continue answering my on-going prayer: 'Lord, soften my heart, break my heart with what breaks yours.' As always, there was so much more yet to come.

Chapter 49

Change Time

It had been cooking for a while. Finally I knew the seasons had changed. It was time for me to retire, to move out and let others carry on leading the church. It was not an easy decision but, over time, the feeling had grown into conviction; this was definitely what heavenly Father had for me. The church was well established, had just passed it's ten year anniversary and could certainly do well without me.

I shared this with Tim, my fellow elder, but he didn't feel he should be the one taking the lead. We both shared it with Roger, who led the New Frontiers team in Cumbria, at the next breakfast meeting we had every couple of months; I don't know if he was surprised with what we both had said or not. He said he would talk with the guy who oversaw the wider New Frontiers churches in the north east and north west of England, to see who was looking to take on the leadership of a different church.

Months passed and there was no one forthcoming. A year passed and still no one. It seemed strange. At one of our breakfast meetings with Roger, Tim surprised me. He said that he now felt that he should take over the reins. Roger agreed that he should, if no one else came forward in the next few months.

But where to now for me? 'Ok, I'm definitely leaving in the next few months.' I was absolutely clear and certain that I would leave Carlisle: to stay in the area would not be fair for Tim and I had a strong sense that God had somewhere else for me. The other thing that I was sure of for certain was that I would not be taking on the leadership of another church, not even as an elder. I was to retire! But where? I now knew when I should finish, at the end of December that year, but that was all I knew.

Other church leaders from our northern region knew about my impending retirement. At one of our regular regional leader's gatherings, John, who had just started a new church in Harrogate, approached me and said that I would be more than welcome, to come and be a part of their recently started church plant in north Yorkshire. That would make sense. It was the same church that my daughter, Hannah, and husband, Dan had moved to a year or two ago, in the early days of that new church. That would be great. I had got to know Harrogate quite well over the last few years, when visiting Dan and Hannah and their little one; they were thriving there, following their move from Carlisle. I thanked John for his welcome invitation.

I drove home over the Pennines with all sorts of thoughts buzzing through my head. It could work so well for me, John was a great young man and very relational. It was so nice to be wanted by someone!

Over the next week, day by day, the idea died on me. No reasons why, but it became a growing conviction that Harrogate was just not right for me. That conviction never left me. I had total peace when I communicated to John, with regret, that I didn't believe it was right for me.

So where would I go then? I'm in no doubt at all that our heavenly Father, by his Holy Spirit, does guide us.

Life carried on much as ever. Summer was on us and where was I to go for my holiday? I decided on two weeks somewhere in Cornwall with my little old caravan. I booked a pitch with the Caravan Club in a village not far from St Austell on the south coast. To my surprise I then found out that Dan and Hannah, with little Sophie, were also booked for two weeks at a caravan site on the edge of St Austell. Their second week overlapped with my first week. Sounded great, we could meet up. Of course, the weather was fantastic and I could get to know Sophie, their little daughter, better as well. And so it happened and it was a great week.

In my second week I decided to pay a visit to the New Frontiers church plant in Truro, which I'd heard, on the grapevine, had been going for a year or so. They were now meeting in a local village hall on Sundays. Teas and coffees were served on the way in and I recognised a couple behind the serving counter; in a previous decade we'd been in the same church. I said hello as the wife handed me a coffee.

The meeting followed the normal New Frontiers model, a time of praise and worship followed by a session of Bible teaching from the main leader. He seemed a very able man. Then of course, there was more coffee on the way out.

As I drove away afterwards, I couldn't get over it. No one had approached me or connected in the slightest way - apart from that question, 'tea or coffee?' at the start and the end. This was definitely not my kind of a church. I couldn't get it out of my head. How sad. I spent the rest of my week exploring more of my forgotten Cornwall. However, for the rest of that week I was strangely disappointed, disturbed and not a little worried with how that church had seemed to be.

For the long slow journey pulling my caravan the 450 miles back home I just couldn't get rid of the thought filling my head that I should move back to Cornwall. Over the next few weeks it didn't fade; in fact the complete opposite was happening. I kept posing the question, 'Father, is this what you've got for me?' The question turned into a conviction that just grew in me: I should move back to Truro and join that New Frontiers church in the city; throw my lot in wholeheartedly and not forget that hard lesson I'd learned fifteen years earlier - from the heart submit to the elders and God will bless!

I was now in no doubt that this was the next step for me. 'Thank you Father.' I spoke over the 'phone and shared what I was feeling about my future with Hannah, and Dan in Harrogate. What a surprise! During their camping holiday in Cornwall those two weeks before, God had independently spoken clearly to them both that they should leave Harrogate, where they were doing so well and move to St Austell in Cornwall, with a definite sense of call: 'The people of St Austell need Jesus.'

I couldn't but laugh. That would be wonderful. What a bonus to have family living closer to me again. I'd never dreamt Hannah would ever go back to Cornwall, let alone St Austell!

Farewell to Kings Church Carlisle
In the first week of December that year I said my final goodbye. A lovely couple had organised a farewell evening at a local venue and invited others from the Cumbria New Frontiers region to join in. They pulled the stops out. There was a video recording of what people thought of me. Glug!! We ate great food and, of course, a large cake. It was so

embarrassing, but I really appreciated it. The future held a tough time for Tim as he took over to lead on his own, but it was so good that he had real faith for God being in it and the strong support of Sam, his wife.

Not surprisingly, I felt a great sadness when saying goodbye to so many wonderful people; many that I'd got to know so well and many who had faced and come through such hard times.

Remembering that time, as I write, and how it had been for me, was also very salutary; there had been so many good things, I'd learned so much, but also made so many mistakes. I knew that I had changed a great deal during my time in Carlisle. It had been years of radical change, in so many ways and in particular I was still adjusting to singleness.

As I faced a brand new year ahead I had much to fill my mind, so much change to achieve, a house to sell, new accommodation to find in Truro, as well as 'what is this retirement business all about?' As the song says, 'If I ever needed you Lord, I need you now.' And I was still young, only sixty. something. The future was certainly looking exciting!

SECTION TWO

Retirement

A New Season Starts

These years of retirement have given the opportunity for so much reflection: joining the dots, and facing up to some of the painful experiences of past years; it's been a real challenge. At times I've felt disregarded because I'm retired. Facing regrets and painful memories have so easily led me to beat myself up: 'If only I'd seen this back then, how differently I would have responded, thought or behaved!'

Without doubt, I've become so aware of how my heart can so easily harden; the cry to 'soften my heart' has been my continued request. Despite it all, the good and the not so good, the patience and grace in practice of my ever present, accepting, heavenly Father, is amazing.

Chapter 50

Return to Cornwall

My return to Cornwall was just over ten years after Sue and I had left there with our two girls at the turn of the millennium. So much had happened during those ten years, and, in so many ways, Cornwall had also changed profoundly.

My son in law, Dan, and my good friend, Fred, from across the street in Carlisle, helped me move. Fred drove the bulging hire van. On arrival at my new house, the three of us unloaded for the start of my new life.

I had a buyer for 7 Lismore Street Carlisle and so was able to purchase a lovely ninety year old semi-detached former council house, with three bedrooms. It came with a garden back and front and was only ten minutes walk from the centre of town; definitely a significant bonus for Truro, it was on the flat all the way!

Re-entry to Cornish life was strange, filled with so many memories, good and bad, sad and even ugly, but it was also wonderful to be back. A whole new way of life had begun. I could get out and take many early morning pre-sunrise images with my fantastic camera. Perched on cliff edges, waiting for just the right shot of glorious sunrises or sunsets, in so many coastal locations was a special treat. I transferred to the local camera club and began to learn so much more about image composition and processing. It was a challenging delight.

Grace Church was growing exponentially. My first Sunday meeting was also the church's first meeting in Truro University's large refectory. There were many people to get to know, especially in the 'small group' that I'd joined. The relatively new church was attracting a large number of students from the Falmouth University. The church was providing the students a weekly bus service from door to door. One of the church members was a driver for a local bus company and the company owner was allowing him to have use of the bus on Sundays to drive the students from Falmouth to Truro and back - at no charge. Amazing.

For me it was a personal challenge to have no responsibility in church life, after so many years. But I knew it was good for me to just fit in and be a part. I knew this is what God wanted me to be doing at that time.

The months and years went by. At the start of the church, Andrew, along with his wife, had been the ones with the vision for a new church in Truro. They had gathered folk from different parts of the UK, all with a background in New Frontiers' churches and a similar vision for Truro and Cornwall. They had all made a very good start. Andrew was the main leader and, at that time, was teaching RE in a Truro private school; he was well equipped with degrees from Cambridge in Biological Sciences, Philosophy and qualifications in Theology. A truly gifted man with a great brain. I remain so jealous of his speed reading skills!

A few months after I had moved and joined Grace Church, Dan and Hannah, along with little Sophie, found a property to rent and moved to St Austell. It was so good to have more family living near by.

Chapter 51

A Very Special Person

One Sunday morning, while I was still at Kings Church, Carlisle, I met a young man, named   James, visiting our morning meeting. Over coffee, at the end of the meeting, James briefly told me a little of his story. He was in his early thirties and had just come back from Dubai. We agreed on a time when he could come to our church office and tell me more.

Although tentative to start with, he seemed to grow in confidence and one thing led on to the next. I listened intently. What a journey this young man had been on!

His upbringing had been tough. Sadly, his mum was emotionally and mentally disadvantaged, so she was not able to cope well with her four children. She lived on the south coast of Scotland with her husband, who was prone to violence towards his wife and children, and, even more so when drunk, which was a regular Friday night happening. Late one Friday night, when dad came home from the pub, the situation was tense. The inevitable row erupted. James' grandmother was in the room when the father went for his wife, waving a large chopper over his head, intent on killing her. Five year old James had taken shelter under the stairs, cowering in terror, as a five year old would. He watched as his grandmother stepped up between husband and wife, finger pointing and yelling above the pandemonium, 'You'll have to kill me first'. The father hesitated, then backed off swearing and cursing his head off.

Bless their hearts, James' elderly grandparents adopted him and one of his brothers. They couldn't cope with the older two brothers as well, so they were taken into care. It was a much needed new start for James and his brother John. Their grandfather was a church pastor and after a few years they all moved from their Scottish homeland a few miles across the border to just outside Carlisle.

Those early years were no easy start to life; they wouldn't be for anyone and they certainly weren't for James and John either. Now living in the little village of Armathwaite by the River Eden was idyllic. The boys attended the village school - most of the time! Boys will be boys. James at the age of ten, along with his mates, took to glue sniffing - how exciting! The sensations, the 'out of it-ness', was risky living and it was so easy! You pop the solvent into the polythene bag and just sniff it, breath it in. Easy. When well experienced, the time came that, oops, James pulled the bag a bit too far over his head, absorbed in the amazing 'experience' and, taken up with it, he passed out before he could get the bag off his head. The inevitable consequence was speedy death. The end of it all. James sat in my office and continued the story.

Re-living that moment, he explained that he hadn't realised he was dying; he was surrounded by a bright light and an angel stood in front of him, who, short and to the point said: 'Jesus has got more for you James!' Then it disappeared. James recovered consciousness in a state of shock and quickly pulled his head from the polythene bag, only then realising that he'd been in a death situation. Was that a dream? But he knew enough about glue sniffing to know that he had been all but dead. He had mates now buried, who'd gone in identical situations.

Understandably, the experience that day was etched into his memory. It made a difference to James' life he stopped glue sniffing, but that was all. His grandfather, the preacher that he was, was always going on about how James must repent, give his life over to Jesus and live differently, but no further change happened. He did, however, change tack by his mid-teens; James became addicted to heroin, easily done once he'd started. They were heart breaking years for his grandfather and grandmother, Nanna. Brother John went down a different road with a developing dependence on alcohol.

Truly horrendous, desperate years for James and the family followed, as James struggled toward his mid-twenties. One afternoon, while in a mindless heroin downer, desperation and despair took hold of James.

Adjacent to Armathwaite village was the railway station; the line crosses over the river Eden on a long viaduct, 100 foot above the fast flowing waters below. The public footpath crossed the river alongside the railway bridge. The thought had been in his head many times before; now was the time to do it. In a semi-conscious state James climbed the fence of the walkway to finally put an end to all this. Enough was enough. He launched himself into thin air; into the deep waters below, it was certain death.

With no idea how long he'd been lying unconscious on the large granite rocks underneath the bridge, James regained consciousness. He'd misjudged it; he hadn't walked far enough into the centre of the bridge and landing on the ugly rocks covered with just a foot or so of water, he was a hairs breath from the deep torrent of the powerful river. Instead of unconscious drowning, while being swept towards the Solway Firth, he'd been knocked out on impact and came to with agonising pain all over his body. Bones were broken and he was experiencing acute pain just trying to breath.

Strangely, James felt he should try to get up and go home. He struggled over the rocks, under the bridge and towards the one hundred steep steps up to the station. It was slow and agonising, hauling himself up a step at a time. There was no one around to help him as there were not many trains on that line. From the station the road went up towards the village. Grandad had died by this time and James lived with Nanna. The terraced house was on the right and it was only two hundred yards more for James to drag himself. But it took him a good forty minutes from the rocks to finally collapse at the front door and bang on it. Bless her heart, Nanna opened the door to James, her blood covered, shivering grandson. It didn't take long for the ambulance to take him away to the Carlisle Infirmary.

It was a cross roads for James. His body slowly recovered and his system was forced to de-tox. A few weeks later he was back with Nanna, recovering and reflecting. That experience when he should have died glue sniffing was ten years before and now his jump to finally finish it all was at the front of his mind. God had definitely intervened that first time and here it was again. He definitively should be dead! The pastor of the local Elim church where Nanna now attended, came to visit James and listened to his story.When strong enough, James decided he would give the church a try, as Nanna was going there anyway.

Transformation

A few weeks later James made a response to follow Jesus. Not untypical for James, he really went for it. He was baptised in water and experienced a profound impact on his life when he was baptised in the Holy Spirit. He was truly transformed: the change was evident for everyone to see - and hear! However, there was a cloud still remaining; that heroin addiction. The pastor worked hard and arranged a place for James with Teen Challenge in Scotland; it would be residential for two or three years.

They were tough years for James, the discipline was very hard. However, it was just the environment he needed. He came through with flying colours finding the freedom to be himself for the first time in his life.

On return to Carlisle, the plan was for him to work in the church, with a view to go to Elim Bible College and full-time ministry. However, as time passed it became clear to James that what the pastor was planning was not the way for him, to the pastor's great disappointment, having invested so much in him.

James explained to me that his uncle and aunt had invited him to live with them in Dubai and he would be able to work in an English speaking church there. He had already been putting his excellent people skills and teaching gift to good use and agreed it would be a good next step.

James also told me that while in Dubai he'd met a young Christian Indonesian lady. They'd hit it off and agreed to get married when visas and all the paper work had been sorted out; in the meantime it was to be a 'phone and internet relationship, as she was going back home to Indonesia.

It was truly a remarkable story that James had shared with me and, in no way did I doubt the account of his journey to date. A few weeks passed and James confirmed that Kings Church was now the place for him.

The years passed and James proved to be a very special 'gift'. He had an outstanding ability in the prophetic and he heard from God with very specific detail for many people. James also had such a passion for Jesus and was bringing so much encouragement to people in our church. During the week he was also doing well as a full time youth worker in a community just outside Carlisle.

A Shadow Remained

After several years the two of us had become close friends, but it became clear to me that a shadow from the past had caught up with James. He was struggling with heroin again. On one occasion he came to my house to stay, in order to go through withdrawal. My house in Carlisle was far enough away from the village where he lived with his grandmother, so it was well out of reach of the dealer who lived just a few hundred yards from where James and Nanna lived. It was a heart rending time, sitting by the bed with the curtains drawn, as he rolled and struggled with the agony tearing his body and mind. I stayed with him, prayed with him and did whatever I could. After two days and nights he said he was better and must get back to look after Nanna. I encouraged him to stay longer and get really established, but he insisted. I feared that the closeness to temptation would be too much.

Life went on. James took a trip to Indonesia and got married to Ike, with the expectation that it would then be easier to get a visa for her to come to the UK as his wife. As the months, then the years passed, James was leading a hard double life a marriage relationship through the internet and yet also day to day living as a single man. There were times when he seemed strange, but he still continued to be a real blessing. He was doing well, keeping his job as a youth worker, and then training in psycho-dynamic counselling. Though James had next to no education, he was a clever guy and was top of his class in the counselling training. But the shadow still lingered.

Chapter 52

A Fresh Start in Cornwall

Though I had now retired and moved back to Cornwall, James and I kept in touch by 'phone many times a week. The heroin cloud was exerting its control on him more and more. It was heart breaking, especially for Nanna; she was in her eighties and spent much of her life in bed with on going heart issues. She remained an incredible support for James.

In desperation, a time came when James agreed to come and stay with me, to escape from the drug dealers and the ready temptation just a few hundred yards down the road. I drove up to Cumbria to bring him back to Cornwall. He was in bad shape, under the influence of what he'd recently injected. With his grandmother present, I laid down my conditions for him to
come back with me: no more drugs, totally open and transparent with me in everything, if it was working then, after an initial period of 6 to 8 weeks, we'd review things for the future. He agreed wholeheartedly. James insisted that I stay out of sight when I went with him to the dealer with the money he owed. Afterwards he told me that he had told the dealer he would not be back. Sorted.

I drove almost non-stop from Carlisle to Truro. James sat in the passenger seat, his eyes closed, writhing in fitful sleep. Once again he was going through agonising withdrawal. The next day, after what he said was a reasonable nights sleep, he was feeling much better. A brand new start had begun. He and I got on well and James settled straight away connecting with the folk in the church. Always the handyman, he volunteered to do some much needed house decoration. Our church small group welcomed him so well and it wasn't long before he was bringing prophetic encouragement and getting involved with people. It felt like he was really finding his feet and rediscovering himself again without the pressures of home territory.

It was Saturday after a couple of weeks; James said he was feeling cooped up. That evening he ventured out to stretch his legs and explore the town. I was more than surprised when he didn't come home later that evening. I got no response on his phone. Eventually, I went to bed more, than a little disturbed.

Early the next morning, I got a 'phone call from James. 'Can you come and pick me up? I'm at the A&E.' I found him in the waiting area - with a black eye and bruised face. He told me his story. He'd gone to a bar and had a great time talking with the people there. On the way back home there was a bunch of people on the pavement outside another bar. One of the men was picking on a lady. James had gone to her defence and the next thing he knew was on the way to the hospital in an ambulance. The police had dispatched him in his unconscious state; his face looked awful and he was still groaning with the pain. He'd spent the rest of that night at A&E, but it was now alright for him to come home.

A couple of weeks later, once again he didn't come home in the evening. Early the next morning I got a call.

James said that he'd been getting on well with his friends in a bar, then one of them suggested they drive out to his place so he agreed to go with them. After a while James said he felt he should be getting home as he was not feeling comfortable with what they were doing. He set out to walk home but had no idea where he was; he was out in the country somewhere. While walking in the dark he'd seen a derelict car and, to get out of the rain, he had slept in it for a few hours. As it got lighter, he saw he was close to a house and took fright at the prospect of being discovered. He set off walking again. Eventually he came to a small village with a village store that was open even though it was still very early in the morning

James called me from the shop 'phone. 'Barry will you please come and pick me up!' I asked him where he was. He had no idea. I told him to ask the shopkeeper. She told him a name and I concluded he was somewhere on the road between St Austell and Newquay, a forty minute drive away. I was committed to setting up the refreshments at the church meeting that morning and told him I couldn't go and fetch him. I said he was on a bus route to St Austell and could get a connection from there back to Truro. He arrived back later that afternoon. If I hadn't realised it before, I was now in no doubt; the problem now was not heroin but alcohol. For my part, I was struggling with the issue of credibility. It seemed to be one thing after another and I was seriously concerned.

It was so ironic, James was so gifted and was such a blessing to those around him, without doubt, more than anybody else I knew and God had still been using him significantly. When he was feeling better the next day we had a heart to heart. Things had to change. We agreed that he would be transparent and accountable to me.

Over the next two weeks he seemed to be doing better. But then I began noticing things. Once again, one night he didn't come home. At eleven o'clock I decided to go and try to find him. I went into all the pubs and bars in the city I could think of, but to no avail. I went home and waited. Eventually he came home the worse for wear. We talked. I told him that I couldn't live with the pressure of the responsibility any longer and that he had to go back. I said I'd put him on the coach back to Carlisle in two days; I was totally gutted, doing this to my special friend, but I felt, rightly or wrongly, that I had no other choice. The morning came when I drove him to the bus station; he didn't utter a word. I watched him board, but still he said nothing. As the coach turned and left, I waved he just looked straight ahead. The morning after he got back to Cumbria I had a 'phone call from Nanna. She had just found James in his bed dead.He'd overdosed that night.

What a Conclusion

I was invited to take the funeral service at the Carlisle crematorium a week later; it was the very least I could do to support Nanna. The day before the service, I travelled to Carlisle. Mel, a lady in my church who had been getting to know James wanted to attend as well, so she joined me on the very long coach trip north.

When I stood at the lectern at the front of the chapel in the crematorium that day I was staggered at the number of people attending. After all the handshakes at the door on leaving, I found out that many were of James' family. I

251

talked to as many of the brothers, aunts, uncles and cousins as there was time for. Most were not Christians but were amazingly open to talk about themselves; so many broken marriages, divorces, alcohol dependencies and sadnesses. Obviously, the context of the day had softened them enough to be able to be so vulnerable with a stranger like me.

Mel and I were invited to refreshments at a a local tea room. The group of ten older folk, including Nanna, welcomed us both so warmly. Most were Nanna's close relatives of her generation. I had a conversation with the aunt James had stayed with in Dubai who now lived with her husband in Cyprus, but he had not been able to make the journey for the funeral. She painted a very different picture of James' stay with them in Dubai than what James had told me. She confirmed what I had come to conclude Ike had never lived in Dubai, in fact she had never travelled outside Indonesia and she had first met James on an internet dating program.

As we made to leave, Nanna pushed an envelope into my hand with money for my coach tickets, as they all warmly thanked me for conducting the service that morning. Mel and I both felt we needed to go and unwind before the long slog the next day in that coach. She went to her B&B and I enjoyed a relaxing evening staying with Fred, my faithful Christian friend who lived opposite where I used to live in Carlisle.

That return trip was salutary for me. So much to reflect on. All those years. Had I been too gullible, accepting all that James had told me? Had I been foolish and irresponsible in inviting him to stay with me in Cornwall? And now I was having to face up to the results. There was so much acute sadness, but there was also the patently dramatic ways in which God had used James. I'd witnessed so many of them over the years. Just before the funeral service had started, I was handed sheets of A4 paper with over forty email responses to the news of James' death, from people around the world. They all had the same testimonies of how God had very specifically spoken to them through what James had spoken to them; these were people who had met James through the internet but never personally.

Then, there was the consuming sadness during that long drive with James to Cornwall. There were so many what ifs. God, why didn't you step in? Since that journey and James' stay with me, I've come to realise the amazing reality - my sadness was just a fraction of the sadness our Father God feels for James, but he would never violate his wonderful gift of choice, given to James and each one of us. If I was able to wind back the clock, I'd still welcome him and seek to encourage him in Jesus as much as I possibly could. I'm in no doubt, James was a very special man and a very special gift of God. I'm thinking that knowing what I now know I would still invite James to come to Truro. Despite all the mistakes I've made, my heavenly Father still welcomes me with open arms and accepts me unconditionally. Maybe I need to learn from his example.

Chapter 53

Argentina

Of great surprise to me, during this time of retirement, was an invitation from a friend, in the church we were both attending. 'I'm making a trip to Argentina in September for a month or so, then moving on to Chile for a further month; how about you join me, Barry, for the Argentine leg? Usually my wife Janet comes with me but she's going to give it a miss this year.'

That was definitely way out of the blue. Peter and Janet had been retired for a few years, after having lived most of their working lives and raising their family in Venezuela. They had been with a Christian mission involved in South America and had seen new churches born and developed over the years, until they had to move from Venezuela to start afresh in Chile. Living now in the UK, they had continued to encourage the churches in Chile, but from a distance with annual visits.

Peter also had contacts in Argentina. The leader of a network of churches in northern Argentina had invited him to visit and minster to the churches that autumn.

What should I do? I didn't speak a word of Spanish, the air flights would cost a fortune and the very idea would be venturing into the totally unknown for me. Peter reassured me that there would be no problem: I would have a translator with me when I was out with the different churches.

I became really excited at the prospect. A month or so later, the two of us were on the long flight to Buenos Aires. In no way was I disappointed. Everything about the trip was completely and wonderfully out of my box!

We were both based in the central church in Corrientes for the first two weeks. There were a surprising number of churches in the Corrientes vicinity and our main speaking appointments were in the evenings. For the first few occasions I went with Peter; he spoke, while I soaked it all in and learnt. Then we went our separate ways. I was allocated a translator and now I was off - into the deep end! It was a terrifying, yet invigorating, experience. I had no option, but to rely on the Holy Spirit, big time.

After those two first weeks, Peter and I moved further north in stages across the Missiones region. Every night, we both went to different churches to speak. During the day, we were taken to visit the variety of ways the churches were serving their communities. I was particularly struck with the way all the churches had such an earnest desire to experience more of the Holy Spirit.

At the end of our stay, as we reached the far north, there was an extra bonus the day we spent exploring the Iguazu Falls. They were most definitely one of the 'Wonders of the World'. The experience was truly amazing, though we had to be willing to get a bit wet! The seven massive waterfalls were in an expansive horseshoe shape and there was rising mist from the powerful spray above each one. It was an awesome experience and my camera was exhausted at the end of that day along with both Peter and me.

We then travelled south on the coach to Buenos Aires. After a couple of days seeing the sights there, it was time for the two of us to part company. Peter caught his flight to Chile and I flew back to the UK.

There was so much to reflect on over the following weeks and months. I was left with a surprisingly consistent impression of the many people we had met. In so many diverse situations, every time we had finished speaking and given the opportunity for prayer ministry, so many people responded.

There was one occasion, with a congregation of two hundred plus, when, after I had spoken, the pastor gave an invitation to respond, and more than half of the congregation flooded to the front of the hall. Each person evidently came with expectation that God would meet with them.

I'm under no illusion that the response might have been due to my erudite biblical exposition, or the manifest power of God on me! These people were hungry and desperate for God to meet with them. The main leader prayed for the whole congregation from the stage while I, with my trusty translator, stepped down from the high stage and literally fought our way slowly through the throng at the front of the hall.

I was confronted again and again with such hungry people, all wanting more of the reality of Jesus in their lives. They had faith for healing, forgiveness and more of him; such passion and urgency was being expressed. It was an overwhelmingly new experience for me. As I pushed my way through the tightly packed crowd of people, they were all trying to get my attention. I was crying out to God, 'Father show me the ones you want me to go to and give me what to say, please'. The time flashed by but there were still people waiting their turn. It was now late and we had to finish. The main pastor and his wife had graciously been waiting in the office for me and the translator, their son, for such a long while and they were going to take me the forty five minute drive back to our base in Corrientes. The caretakers had also been waiting patiently to finally close the building and get home.

Significant food for thought: these people and so many others that I encountered over those four weeks, had such different expectations from those I was used to. It was not just head understanding and learning they were wanting and expecting, but heart connection and the outworking of who Jesus is, and has promised in their lives and the lives of their families.

I returned from my Argentine adventure significantly stirred. There were certainly elements that were not for me but, also, significant challenges to my expectations and confirmation of areas that were cooking in my life: 'You've got so much more for your Church on this earth, haven't you heavenly Father, if only we will be willing to welcome it.'

Chapter 54

The Next Step

It was truly so good being back in Cornwall. Cumbria was also a privileged place to live. North, south, east and west, there are so many wonderful unspoilt outdoor areas to explore, walk and photograph. My little caravan proved to be a wonderful God-send making it so easy to be able to escape the pressures of work for a few days, into areas with few people spoiling the panoramas! Five years on and Grace Church had been growing well. The 'small group' I was a part of was very special. Genuine relationships were developing over the months and years; lives were being touched and changed.

However, the years passed and I was being stirred once again. Maybe God had a further step for me? It was a gradual process, as the stirring developed into a growing conviction.

I was especially challenged reading the New Testament writers' encouragement and correction of those newly established churches. Revisiting the records of how the early church had developed and spread over the first century across much of the then known world, was significantly challenging. I'd always liked church history and have always believed that we have so much to learn from the early years of church experience, for good or the not quite so good. There had been wonderful growth and expansion but, also, so much tragedy and godless practices slipping in. What developed over the second and third centuries in particular, sadly, shaped and validated what came to be known as legitimate 'tradition'.

There was another factor I was realising more and more: the dramatic rate of change in our culture now, that is all around us. There is so much affluence and yet, exponential dissatisfaction; so much despair and, sadly, at the same time, what is seen as the widespread irrelevance of the church today. Tradition is ceasing to carry the weight it once did - maybe, just maybe, this is God's opportunity!

More and more, the patently desperate need for the reality of Jesus and what only he can provide, is being realised by some; the possibility of experiencing a 'vibrant church', with the central experience of personal transformation and relationship, with the living, miracle-working Jesus. Surely this and church expressed as family, with real relationship, has to be more than a dream?

At this time of stirring, my daughter, Hannah, had shared with me that she and Dan had a growing conviction that God's call to them for the people of St Austell was moving to a new stage. They were feeling that they should be moving their church life to where they lived, in St Austell rather than Truro. Over the previous few years, they had experienced amazing God interventions in many of their neighbours' lives and also with Dan's work clients. Both had been praying for people to be healed, with some wonderful answers. In response, one lady had given her life to Jesus.

It is so noteworthy that those who were open to listen and willing to be prayed for, were those who were struggling and in desperate need. The relevance of those 'signs' that Jesus had performed and also had been experienced in the early church, made an impact then - quite understandably. It's the same today, God still gives and wants to give, significant pointers, or signs, to the reality of the living, active Jesus.

The time came when Dan and Han, with their two kids, stood before Grace Church one Sunday morning and said their farewell. I joined with them that day convinced that I too, should be joining with them and supporting them in what God had for St Austell in the days ahead.

Chapter 55

Fascinating Swans

Another of the great advantages of being back in Cornwall and having more time to get out and about, is the amount of water that is all around. Not just the sea, north, south and west, but oodles of rivers, creeks, estuaries and marsh areas.

There's one creek, miles inland from the sea, that I drive along regularly on my way to another town. There's a 30 mile an hour speed limit on this stretch, so I can get a quick glance or two, as I drive by. There they are again on the opposite bank - those two swans. They are such a familiar sight along this creek. Further downstream there's a footpath alongside the river that runs for several miles. At different times of the year, when walking up or down the river, one can see those two swans.

Into the summer there are another two smaller swans, the next generation, carefully keeping close to mum and dad. I've checked up, swans as well as several other birds, keep their relationships and mate for life.

Watching these swans got my mind working. Us humans are also born to relate, in so many different ways. Where does this come from? Of course it starts with our Creator God, with his Son, Jesus and the Holy Spirit. Wonderfully, human beings have been created in the image of this one true God. The source of relationship in our world and especially for us, is an expression of the relationship within the Trinity.

Jesus demonstrated relationship, par excellence, during his life on this earth. The Gospels give us the record: Jesus related in a very special way with all sorts of people: the rich, the poor, the broken, the arrogant and the hopeless. Jesus could engage and connect, with everyone who came across his path, those who welcomed him but also those who spurned him. 'People is people', we all come in different shapes and sizes, as was then, it's no different now.

Time has taught me that not everyone is like me; those that know me will say 'thank heavens' and I agree! Late in life I've come to realise that I am quite relational. For the longest time people not like me have been a great puzzle. I learnt so much from my friend Colin, who I referred to earlier, a consummate introvert. Just as the apostle Paul gives us the great picture of the Church being like a body, with many differing parts, just so, these parts relate differently, as is natural for them, according to how God intends and has made them.

Transferable Tips

For those for whom relating and making the running towards other folk doesn't come naturally or easily, I've been able to pass on a few of the keys, that have come my way.

The starting place is making the choice. Choice is an intentional decision, whether easy or unnatural. It takes practice, and as we know 'practice makes perfect' or, if not perfect, it can certainly bring a growing confidence and effectiveness as we do it, in something that may not come naturally or easily for us.

Tip One: Ask Questions. Not pointed or intensely personal
questions to start with. Pose questions that will give the other person the opportunity of talking, in their comfort area. Nine times out of ten you'll be surprised at how willing the other person to talk - about themselves.

Tip Two: Listen! Listen to the person with your ears and also listen to the person with your eyes. Body language and attitude is reflected in tone of voice and facial expression; so listen to that body language. Of utmost importance at this stage is to 'shut up!' Listen and do not be quick to add your response or opinion.

Tip Three: Depending on how the conversation is going, respond by seeking to identify with what is being told you with a similar connection, experience or feeling. If it seems appropriate, a more personal or a deeper question will often work. I find the easiest thing to do is to talk too much of my experiences, when I'm seeking to identify with the person. When I do, I apologise!

Tip Four: Be prepared. Quite possibly, your new 'friend' will not ask questions about you. Just possibly, next time you meet the person, after asking how he's been getting on, it may just be appropriate to say a little about yourself. For myself, I know I must not rush it and not worry if there isn't opportunity for me to speak about myself. I must be willing and content to keep my 'wisdom' to myself.

This is all part of building a relationship with someone, anyone, whether a follower of Jesus or not yet; whether introvert, extravert, or any other vert.

We have all been created for relationship and all relationships have to be started and then built. It goes without saying, that an introvert is also created to build relationships!

Chapter 56

Abide in Christ

So many times I've heard the comment, 'How does this Christianity thing work? I just don't get it!' I must confess, it's the same question I've posed many times too. Maybe you have as well.

When I was in my first year as a student, one of the third year students, whose room was at the other end of the corridor, introduced me to a book that he was very excited with. His enthusiasm, along with his explaining some of it's gems, made obtaining a copy a must for me too. The bookstall in the Christian Literature Crusade HQ was just up the road in Upper Norwood and they had a copy.

I started straight away reading one chapter each day, taking it slowly. It was all about the title, 'Abiding in Christ'. The book was based on what Jesus told his disciples, as recounted in John's Gospel chapter 15. Of course, I'd read that chapter many times, but this was now different. It began to come alive for me. So simple, so straight forward, well of course it was obvious. But what did it all mean for me in my life?

The directive and encouragement of the verb 'to abide' in this passage, is in the present continuous tense, endorsing the reality of this to be an ever ongoing experience, one second at a time. It is noteworthy, that the English translation of the Greek word is simply to 'remain'.

Jesus paints the word picture of a vine with branches, for the sole purpose of growing great grapes!

'I am the true vine, and my Father is the vinedresser. (v 1)
I am the vine; you are the branches. Whoever abides in me and
I in him,
he it is that bears much fruit, for apart from me you can do nothing.'
(v 5)

All I have to do is remain in Christ. Wonderful. This is success or failure in the Christian life. I was certainly up for it. After all those teenage years of trying to be good, reading my Bible with the Daily Notes, witnessing and generally doing the right things this is so straight forward! Jesus teaches his disciples something so simple - I'm to just remain in Christ, where he has put me, based solely on who he is and what he has done *'. . . you have died, and your life is hidden with Christ in God.'* writes Paul in Colossians chapter 3 verse 3.

I believed it and I tried to do it. Great! But, it didn't seem to work. Was I just passive in this thing? What was I supposed 'to do' that is so different from what I've been doing all along; before this came up?'

The Missing Part

It was a long while before I began to make the essential connections: the Helper, as John in his gospel, refers to him in Chapters 14, 15 and 16, is the Holy Spirit. He is the 'paraklete' the *called alongside* one, as the Greek word literally means. Jesus then goes on to explain the part that the Holy Spirit plays: We can do nothing without him! John understood it completely; only in total reliance on the strength, enabling and power of the Holy Spirit can we remain in Christ Jesus, in total dependence on him.

I have a vital part to play; passivity does not work. Knowing my inability to do it and facing up to my weakness, I must choose. And here it is again the 'Big C'. Moment by moment I must depend on the Holy Spirit. Surprise, surprise: when I intentionally make that choice to depend on him and trust him, it is different!

Those were very early days for me, good seed was sown, but there was so much more I had to experience and mistakes to make. Those months were part of a profound learning adventure which I am still on to this day. One day, one hour, one moment at a time. Thank you, Andrew Murray, for what you saw in the late nineteenth century and wrote in your book 'Abide in Christ', all those years ago.

By the way, it's still in print, and in more modern language as well.

Chapter 57

Mistakes! I've Made Only a Few?

Back then I couldn't help but hear it on the radio when milking the cows and I hated the whole tenor of the words and the arrogance with which Frank Sinatra sang the whole song, 'My Way', written by Paul Anka. The final punch line was the worst '. . . I did it my way!' Strangely, a couple of the lines of this song have so often come back to me even though I hate its conclusion.

'Regrets, I've had a few
But then again, too few to mention
I did what I had to do, I saw it through without exemption
I planned each charted course, each careful step along the byway
And more, much more than this, I did it my way.'

The song writer is reflecting on his life and I'm doing the same. I've got so many regrets, not just 'a few'. Wouldn't it be great if my mistakes were things I'd left behind when I reached adulthood? That has definitely not been the case for me!

The more I take the time I now have and re-visit my decades past and many different places I've lived in, I've come to realise that I have learnt so much through the mistakes made! I think I've grown and matured. I now like to hope that my thinking, behaviour, and actions have changed profoundly as a result of all my many mistakes. So often they've been costly, painful and so hard to face up to.

Diamonds only form under great pressure, the most costly and the very best only form with the most extreme pressure and time. No, I'm not saying I'm a valuable diamond! It's the significance of how our wonderful God can take those hard and painful times, and especially the mistakes and regrets we've made, and turn them to good.

The dawning of this realisation is so exciting: what we learn through our mistakes are the most important lessons in our lives. They are not just learnt with our head, they are lessons that can change us, sometimes at the deepest levels. In humility, with heavenly Father's assistance, facing up to our painful mistakes can become truly life changing, with no room for pride or arrogance.

A quote I've now used so often is, 'The lessons that impact us the most are the result of our biggest mistakes.'

A Really Big One

One profound regret I really struggled with was when I was an elder in Kings Church Carlisle at a time when things were going well in so many ways. Tim had joined me as an elder by this time and several families had joined us over the years from other churches in the wider area, bringing with them experience in different aspects of leadership along with their variety of gifting. Two of them in particular had significant experience in their God-given prophetic gifts.

My objective was to draw a wider range of gifted people into playing their part in shaping and growing the church. Sunday gatherings were excellent for the variety of people participating; bringing words of knowledge, the prophetic, praying for healing and general encouragement.

I was convinced that we had to grow our leadership team in order to move forward. To this end, Tim and I were now meeting up regularly with three guys in particular. I felt God was giving me a vision for how he would have us, as a church, serve and reach out to the many communities which made up Carlisle, even more effectively than we were already doing. Carlisle is especially distinctive for the many different communities; each had a significant sense of identity, often revolving around the community centres, pubs and recreational facilities in their district. Many Carlisle people had lived in the same small area for generations. The six or seven home groups that we now had were already meeting in some of these different Carlisle communities. However, there were still many others we could be reaching. I shared my vision, to impact our city even more than we were doing, with Tim. We set a date to share it with the other three guys.

We all met up and off I went with all the enthusiasm I felt. Along side our Sunday meetings, I described a way forward to reach all of Carlisle through our home groups. I was illustrating it on the white board. The home groups could be made up of all the church people who were already living in a particular community. The objective would be to continue to encourage one another in our christian walk, but also to intentionally connect with neighbours and contacts in our community.

I continued: we could start with the group leaders who after catching this vision, would share it with their group, begin praying together for their community, and then invite their contacts to group social events with a vision to seeing the people of their community come to know Jesus as Saviour and Lord. There could then be a relational context for the group members, discipling newcomers and seeing them introduce their family and friends to Jesus in due course. In the longer term, we could be multiplying the groups across the whole Carlisle area and maybe beyond! For me this could work in the medium term but also be an exciting vision for the future.

I paused. 'Ok guys, what do you think?' Silence followed, then, 'Well it's not the way I would do it,' came one response. It landed on me like a ton of bricks. I was totally taken aback at what seemed to be an out of hand dismissal. I looked at the others. Silence. No response at all. I looked to Tim for some support. Nothing. I was totally mortified. That was it. I didn't know what to say. I'd expected questions, lots of them, some discussion with exploring the possibilities. Where could I go from here?

I wound up the meeting. Everyone went home. I felt I was left to lick my wounds.

That evening made such a deep impression on me. Eventually that team came to an end and Tim and I just carried on.

It took many years for me to begin to come to a clear conclusion: that evening became one of my biggest regrets! I had brought too much that seemed to be challenging the prevailing concepts of leadership and practice. I expected them to follow my lead, even if it was a radical vision, or at least to be willing to explore it.

When push came to shove, I did not genuinely 'love' my brothers in the way that Jesus taught and put into practice with his disciples. What I shared that evening was so obvious and workable for me surely it was just an extension of what groups were already doing. But I came away so hurt. I had not taken the time to win them to the potential of my vision for the way forward.

How foolish I'd been. My insecurity was exposed and I didn't face it when I had the opportunity. I'd also fallen into the alluring trap of putting activity and achievement before life and relationship. Maybe most revealing of all, I had assumed a fallacy of church leadership; I was the lead elder, they should follow my lead it's what's expected! Sadly I had been exercising that 'Big C', control.

The years that followed dogged me with such regret after that night. It took a long time, but eventually it has been so good to face up to the false reality reflected in the words of that song.

'Regrets, I've had a few
But then again, too few to mention'

I am so thankful that finally. I've come to terms with the reality that I've made many mistakes. The saying is true, 'he who doesn't make mistakes doesn't make anything' Just maybe, there's a good side to my having to change the last words of that song:

'Regrets, I have so many
Sadly, too many to mention'

Chapter 58

Challenging a Hard Heart

'Change my heart, O God, Make it ever true
Change my heart, Oh God, Make it ever new
You are the potter, I am the clay
Make me and mould me, this is what I say'

During our time at Kings Church in Cornwall God was definitely doing amazing, totally different things. At some stage, during the extended time of worship, I was lying on the floor of the main hall of Redruth Comprehensive School, Sunday after Sunday. For those many months, it wasn't just me. God was evidently doing many different things with so many of the people there at that time. For me, during that period, it wasn't just 'that' floor - whenever and where ever I was, in a meeting or on my own at home, I couldn't help but fall on the floor in a time of praise, worship or seeking God! Logically it seemed so strange; bizare, you may rightly say and so un-British!

However, something very real was happening with me. I was coming to realise that my loving, heavenly Father was starting where the need was greatest my heart. 'Soften my heart, Lord' was my cry of desperation as I lay on the floor with an unstoppable flow of tears. It was with sincere intent, even though I didn't really understand what I was actually asking for, let alone what it would entail. The obvious, correct implication was that I must have a 'hard' heart. Surely not? I didn't see myself like those wretched followers of Moses in the wilderness on their flight from Egypt. They hardened their hearts. Yes, I understood that for them but I was not like them!

Reflecting since that period of time has been interesting. I remember those earliest years, in my high chair next to my mother, holding out my hand to her and sobbing. Then, years later, as a pre-teen, sitting around the family tea table on a Sunday afternoon and again holding out my hand to be held by my mother, while I was crying for no reason that I can remember. I'd not been told off for anything and there was nothing wrong with the food! Doesn't it seem rather strange? Surely I should have grown out of that stuff by then!

What I did pick up at those times, that made a profound impression on me, were the looks of disapproval coming from my father at the other end of the table, to be met with my mother's response of, 'there, there, it's alright Barry,' while gently stroking my hand.

I now realise the significance of what was happening back then; I was being me! I had emotion in me and I was just expressing it in a way that was a natural, real and tangible way for me.

Sadly, however, I was learning. Disapproval can be a powerful and often insidious tool. I was learning how not to behave, what was not appropriate. That was just the beginning of my discovering the power of the 'approval trap', through experiencing and feeling disapproval, along with it's shame. In time, I learnt that lesson well. Learning what was not appropriate and, therefore, how not to behave. Also, what was valued, right and proper! I was a boy. Yes, and, 'Be a man!' How many times did I hear that value expressed over the years. Inevitably I learnt it, to my loss. It meant being strong! We play rugby!

I'm not sure that I heard it said quite like that, but I certainly learnt the lesson and learnt it well. Expressing emotion is a sign of weakness! 'Big boys don't cry'. Later there was even a pop song in the early sixties with its title lauding that truth, 'Big boys don't cry'!

Hand in hand with 'being strong' was its cousin: achieving. I'm from a Bible-believing, passionate for Jesus, family. However, culture wields a powerful pressure and it's so easy not to recognise it for its 'subtle control' of our lives, which, in years to come, can work against so much of the practice, desire and heart of Jesus. None of us are immune, certainly not me, and so often, we naively believe that the choices we have made are on the basis of our reasoned thinking and free choice.

I had no idea in those years that much of what was happening to me then, was reshaping my heart.

Shaped by Parents

My dad was a wonderful man, with a heart of gold. He had a passion for following Jesus, with nothing but integrity and good intentions. As the years passed, I found out more of the unspoken areas of his upbringing and experiences. His family experienced so much heartbreak; dad's father died at a relatively young age from a cerebral haemorrhage, in large part, the result of unthinkable family pressures, made worse with his father's brother committing suicide by jumping under a train at Wimbledon train station. The well established large family business had been failing, at high cost, as a consequence of the Great Depression during the late nineteen twenties. My father was just sixteen. With heartbreaking disappointment, my father had to give up his education along with his prospects of university, which had been so close, in order to get a job. He was now the only bread winner for his mother, who'd never worked in her life and also his younger sister, still at a private school. There was no social welfare system in those days.

A few years later dad had no choice and was off to serve for the next six years in the Royal Corps of Signals, for the duration of the Second World War. Like so many others he was seeing and experiencing the horrendous effects of war. Day two of the Normandy landings was such an awful experience. The advance into France, pushing back the German forces, was just as bad. Everyone had a high price to pay, even if they didn't pay with their lives; my father was no exception. I doubt that the consequences of those years and those that followed ever left him. Post Traumatic Stress Syndrome didn't exist in those days, it was just called a nervous breakdown which was, of course, never to be mentioned. It was a shameful thing to admit to!

No Choice. A Hardening of the Heart

As I grew up and experienced more of the world, I was unaware that long term effects of striving to succeed and the drive to adapt and survive, were squeezing something out of me and, at the same time, replacing it with something else. There's something built into all of us and I'm no exception.

When the wonderful, soft and vulnerable parts of ourselves are challenged, we have to fight and compensate, in order to cope. Of course, in those early years we are not able to reason it through and fight the challenge that our culture tells us we must do to succeed. However there is a price to pay. Some of those soft parts of us are beginning to harden and in due time recede totally, disappearing from our character. It's the normal and natural consequence of being in our fallen world.

Wonderfully, there is . . .

Jesus was different. Jesus, the Son of God came, was born of a human woman and lived among people like us, one hundred percent human in all ways. Jesus also completely reflected the nature of his Father in heaven. Amazing!

To know what God the Father is like - look at Jesus. Jesus is the exact image. Even for us today, this Jesus is made living and real by his Holy Spirit! How about this for a bold statement, and it's true: God in heaven has a 'soft heart' towards us people on this planet, whom he created! If we want to see and know what that looks and feels like, look at Jesus this is softness of heart. As we read the narratives by the Gospel writers, we see demonstration after demonstration of Jesus' softness of heart towards all those who came across his path, through healings and meeting the need of so many desperate people. On occasions, Jesus wept in public at what he saw of people's misery; he was seeing and connecting to the bitterness, hatred and pain of so many people yet at the same time, feeling all that his heavenly Father was feeling in these situations: consummate compassion and heartbreak for people without hope. Sadly, there were so many people who resisted all that he had to offer.

I'm now proud of my earthly father, as I have come to understand some of what he lived through and the pain that shaped his life. My dad also had the gracious hand of his loving and accepting heavenly Father upon him. Wonderfully, this Father has the ability, through what Jesus has done, to accept me too, unconditionally despite all my mistakes, and without doubt the same can apply to you as well!

Now I'm certain over my many years, that my oh so gracious heavenly Father, has been committed to helping me back towards this soft heart of Jesus, into the image of God and the way he created Adam and Eve right at the very start. He has been working at it in me for so many years, and there's so much more softening to be done!

Chapter 59

What is this Heart thing?

Before we go any further we need to clarify what is meant by 'heart'.

What bit of me is my heart? Starting with the obvious, the best picture is understanding the metaphor of the place and part that the heart plays in our body. The heart pumps the blood and serves all areas of our physical body. Every part of us must have that blood to function and we also must have every part of our body functioning in order to survive. When this heart begins to malfunction there is very good reason to panic and get to A&E, quickly!

We refer to the heart in two different ways. In the first instance it's this wonderful physical organ essential for the function of every part of us. We also use the word 'heart' to speak of the very essence of our being. It's a picture of something we can't quite put a physical finger on, but seems to be the deep, the very special 'us'; the combination of our feelings, passions, convictions and aspirations. The Old Testament writers used the word very often in this way for the sum total of our desires, attitudes and feelings, resulting in how we react and behave. They also used the word 'soul' in a similar way. 'Heart' and 'soul' are used interchangeably in the Old Testament.

The New Testament writers, writing in the koine Greek language, used the word 'psuchay', translated 'soul', to describe the same concept as in the Old Testament.

Interestingly, the Old and New Testament writers expressed the same understanding of the nature of mankind: it is tripartite, Body, Soul and Spirit. Some well known Greek philosophers agreed, others disagreed and said, 'No, we're bi-partite, having only two parts'.

This third word, 'spirit', introduces the concept of the God element. In the biblical narrative of God's creation, what set man apart from the rest of the animal world, was that He breathed his Spirit into Adam and he became a 'living being' and able to communicate with Creator God.

All went well until man exercised his God-given gift of choice and went against what God had expressly stated. The result was a breaking of the relationship between man and his Creator God. However, this spirit of special life remained in man but without the very thing he was created for - an intimate, personal and two-way relationship with God, his Creator. As a result, man would never be able to experience the total fulfilment that he was made for, unless something very radical broke what now became the status quo.

Hence, the 'heart' of us, is the sum and total of who and what we are: the expression of our 'soul' plus our 'spirit', all in the setting of our body. In practice, it's the whole of who we are, expressed in the way we think, behave and experience our feelings, for example, attitudes, arrogance, superiority, self-confidence, inferiority, low self-esteem and so much more. All these things result in the way we act and behave.

A hard heart is one that is set; a person who sees him or herself as sorted and in control, convinced that this is the way he must be, along with all the consequences. A softened heart results in us being entreatable and welcoming all that our Creator longs to change within us, so that we may be tender towards people, situations and, most of all to God.

Chapter 60

A Broken Heart

Going back to the 1990s and those quite unusual and strange times, lying on the floor and crying out to God through my tears, 'soften my heart, Lord', and then a month later, 'Break my heart Lord . . . with what breaks yours.' This addition was even more puzzling to me than the original. How could a holy, all powerful, sovereign God, creator of all things - how could he have a broken heart?

Amazingly, it is absolutely true. We are created in his image which means that God has emotion, feelings, the experience of disappointment and loss, just as we do - but to the nth degree. As he surveys the world that he put mankind onto, with the charge *'be fruitful and multiply and fill the earth'* our Creator God is heartbroken. (Gen 1:28)

This relational God was heartbroken over the way his chosen people responded in the wilderness. From then on, because he wanted more than separation from humankind, he sent his much loved, only Son, Jesus who had been an integral part of him since before time, and allowed him to go through all that he did, during his time on earth. God, the Father, was intimately and painfully involved with the desperation of his Son that night in the Garden of Gethsemane, when he had to turn his face away from the cries, *'Father, if you are willing, remove this cup from me. Nevertheless,*

not my will, but yours, be done.' And being in agony Jesus prayed more earnestly; and his sweat became like great drops of blood falling down to the ground'. (Lk 22:42,44).

Truly heart breaking for any father.

How sad that through the ages and right now, knowing all the potential for mankind, when the choice on offer is for total forgiveness and a fresh relationship with their creator, through what Jesus has done for them, people still turn away and continue down the road to hell. This breaks God's heart. Seeing the consequences of self-centred living and the choices that damage and destroy the men and women that he created to experience his boundless love and approval, with the subsequent pain and despair of destroyed lives, across the years: God's heart breaks.

'Break my heart Lord . . . with what breaks yours.'

It is so easy to get taken up with my own bubble. There are challenges enough with my own relationships, my children and my wife. But there are also my wider friendships - the people I work with and certainly my neighbours. That's the reason I now see the absolute need for me . . . and maybe even you, to cry out: 'Break my heart Lord . . . with what breaks yours.'

However, would I really be willing, if I truly understood what it would cost me: the changes that would have to take place in the deepest parts of me? Of course, it was so easy to say, 'Yes' in the awe of those moments, but I am so thankful that he gave me the opportunity of choosing and then longing for him to begin to do it in me; to make the changes in me that I would never have imagined would be necessary, regarding my pride, arrogance, self-sufficiency and very real heartlessness for others.

The decades have passed and it's still my ongoing prayer. It is absolutely essential that I choose to depend on the Holy Spirit
to keep showing me, in the light of Jesus, what I am really like and to help me in the moment to be different. However, even now, I feel that I have only just started along this road. I have to start again every day!

Chapter 61

Satisfied with Harder or Softer?

Just as the children of Israel in the wilderness had a choice, I also have the same choice - all the time. Mighty man that I am, will I live from *my* knowledge, *my* experience and confidence, or will I face my pride, self confidence and total failure at living God's way and come to his feet choosing total dependence on his way, power and enabling? The first way will continue to harden my heart. The second, begins its much needed softening.

The sad thing is that, in our human condition, it is so hard to recognise that we have this problem. Everything we have been taught and which society endorses as being good and essential to succeed in life, results in us never knowing that this way of living hardens our heart in our relationship with God. Though 'born again' of the Spirit of God and walking with him enthusiastically, we can be blind to the 'softness' of heart that he intends for us. Reliance on self is incompatible with the depth of relationship he holds out to us!

The attention grabber for me was those days on the floor with hours weeping out to God. I became acutely aware that there was an option of a hard heart or a soft heart, even for me as a long time follower of Jesus. That time on the floor was so much of a God thing that I couldn't miss that he had something different for me - softer heart and a different relationship with him!

Without doubt, 'the doorway' God had for me was coming face to face with my failures! So many mistakes made, bad choices and lost opportunities; genuinely hearing God's way forward, but then setting off in my own strength. Many times I was taking the proven route; even going with altruistic motives for the glory of God, the building of his church, with a genuine Godly desire to encourage people in their walk with Jesus - but in my own strength! Whether the results were good or bad, the effect for me - for my heart, was hardening. More and more, I was managing quite fine without him, thank you! However, there is a low ceiling on all this. Oh, why has it taken me so long to see it? As ever, our wonderful Father is *'so gracious, slow to anger, and abounding in steadfast love and faithfulness.'* (Exodus 34:6).

I think I'm now gradually getting it. At least I've made a start and it's never too late. It's like breathing! Each breath is fantastic, but the next one must follow! It's an ongoing relationship with the Father, through Jesus, only possible with my dependence on his Holy Spirit. It works like breakfast, lunch and tea - every day. Throughout the day, I have the moment by moment choice: 'Father, soften my heart, right now. Fill me afresh with the life and power of your Spirit so I can truly walk with you!

However, a puzzle still remained that I am now beginning to understand. *'Break my heart with what breaks yours.'* - what does the answer to that cry really mean for me? If I can begin to see and feel what breaks God's heart when he looks on the world he created, the fallen state of the people he has put into this world and especially the condition of his church today, maybe, just maybe, he can use me and others whose hearts are beginning to break with what breaks his heart.

No mean feat! My heavenly Father was taking on the task of reversing the effect of what the years have done to the soft heart he originally created in me. It's exactly the way you too started, with a soft heart! Now, finally, I'm seeing it. I want more of that change - bring it on. And he has been. He's been using all that I saw Sue going through, to impact me during those, oh, so sad, months. I was rediscovering the wonderful, mighty power of emotion. Not denying what's in me, but welcoming it and re-building shattered empathy. Connecting with and acknowledging my weaknesses, my failures, and welcoming the realisation that I was not created to make it on my own and come out 'the strong one'. Rather, discovering that when I face my need, room is made for what I am actually created for - a dependent partnership with my Creator. Oh, the true liberation! Beginning to walk, talk and breath in dependent relationship with Jesus, by the enabling power of his Holy Spirit in me.

My word, he is softening my hard heart of self sufficiency. Three things are beginning to happen. I'm beginning to see myself so differently - it's wonderful; I'm seeing this gigantic, Creator God in a whole different, intimate, personal way, impacting everything about me. I'm seeing people in a whole different way, and beginning to connect and demonstrate, in some small way, something that is absolutely of my heavenly Father.

Chapter 62

Wonderful Realisation

It has taken me such a long time to realise: it seems to be the way God has made me. I like talking to people. It's natural for me to make the running, to start a conversation with something humorous - light hearted or to ask a question and seek an opinion. Even just saying 'hello', with a smile! It's been a 24 carat gold discovery - ninety nine out of a hundred people want to talk - it's just that no one gives them the opportunity. When they have the opportunity it is so surprising where it goes so often. I'm so thankful for my early days on the clinical theology course I took the summer after I graduated from College.

That was just the start of discovering the relational key: to listen. I don't mean 'just listen', I mean really listen and engage in the listening. People tell you things they don't say, through their eyes and their demeanour! So, so often it's sadness: sadness out front or hidden sadness, which when it does come out, comes through with even greater pathos, due to it normally being unspoken. There is so much hidden sadness, heartbreak, hopelessness and despair. I am absolutely certain that this is not what our God has created us people for. God's heart breaks over his mind-blowingly wonderful creation, in which mankind is his 'piece de la resistance'! Here's the proof: *'For God so loved the world that he gave his only beloved son, so that . . .whoever . . .',* that you and I should begin to know his heart, even if just to a minute degree and also, that we his children, may come to feel his heart for the people around us.

I think I am beginning to feel some of his broken heart for us all. Hearing people's stories, being touched and affected by their pain and despair, without adding criticism or arrogance on my part, without trying to fix people with a cheap Elastoplast - it's beginning to affect my heart too. Thank you Father that I am beginning to weep when people's pain begins to touch me deep inside - just a mere shadow of how broken your heart is.

But I know there is so much more I need more of your heart Father. 'Break my heart Lord . . . with what breaks yours.' I've a feeling that it has been happening in me; some seemingly irrational responses to people who are so offensive, who are lost causes or just plain nasty and totally unredeemable - and yet maybe, just maybe, our heavenly Father's heart breaks for them especially. 'To be willing and to be able to see people, all people, the way that you see people, Lord. What must you yet do with me, Lord, so I can begin to feel the way you feel towards people who are the love of your life?'

The Connection

It took a long while, but finally the connection was dawning for me. Our amazing heavenly Father desires to take each of us down the road that is perfect for us. For me, tears well up at what seems to be the slightest thing. So strange, but maybe not when I remember those times in that high chair as an infant and also those pre-teen years; those seemingly irrational tears and needing to feel the touch of my mother.

I'm convinced this is not just for me but it's for all followers of Jesus. 'It's all very well for you Barry, but I'm different from you' I hear you say. Yes, that may be true, but we all have this 'Big C', the gift of choice. We can all learn and operate in areas that are not natural for us. We have to be willing, learn, and then start to do it, depending on his Holy Spirit to enable us. This area may be more natural for me, but, for me, but I need to depended on the Holy Spirit just as much as everyone else. Maybe the only difference for me is that it's an area in which I can be a signpost!

Chapter 63

My Two Fathers

I like to think that my earthly father was the one who conceived me with my mum through a moment of passion and delight!

My dad was very special. He was a child of his times and, in his teens he'd gone through the aforementioned family distress, pain and shattered dreams, only then to have to face the onset of war. Wonderfully, he had served in the army from the first days of the Second World War and then survived those long days of the Normandy landings; later rising through the ranks to become a major.

It was my dad who bought me my first tricycle; I remember it so well. It was all metal with a red seat and, of course, with that great little 'ding ding ding' metal bell, plus those solid rubber tyres that skidded round the corners, almost coming off as I peddled up and down and round and round the small patio at the back of the house. Such good memories for a four-year old.

Dad was very important to me. He was a good man. Sometimes what is painful can also still be good. Without doubt, dad was also an ardent follower of Jesus.

At thirteen, I passed the school entrance exam by the skin of my teeth. It had been an absolute *must* to pass that exam. Then, what a surprise, what a reward. Dad took me to a bike shop; I was allowed to choose a new 'proper' bike with big wheels - and gears! I was now in a new world. I was allowed to cycle the ten miles each way to school and back for the rest of that summer term. It was so exhilarating, and what a sense of freedom. The daily two way journey, six days a week, on those Thanet main roads, was dangerous and totally exhausting, but I loved it.

However, my memory was still seared by those pre-teen years when at the end of each term, those wretched school reports had arrived. They were dreadful evenings. Father came home and the inevitable 'talking to' finally happened. Those words in the report are indelibly etched into my psyche - 'He could do better', followed by the inevitable response, 'Oh Barry, if you don't improve . . .' I learnt the lesson well and it lived with me for so many years: 'I was a failure . . .' Deep inside I felt it, knew it and believed it. The disapproval of my earthly father and with it, of course, the disapproval of my heavenly Father as well.

It may seem strange, though I'm pretty sure it is true that my Dad probably was proud of me as later years passed, but he never expressed 'it'. He never told me. I grew up, got my Honours Degree, found a wonderful wife, had some great kids for him to be a proud grandfather of but I felt that he never really endorsed me.

Fortunately, I had moved on and was fully assured in my inner-self by Sue, my wonderful wife, and our challenging kids. I also kept my passion for Jesus and his church. However, I still believed and carried that inner, hidden weight of disapproval.

For good or ill, what we all grow up with can have a profound influence on us and shape the rest of our lives. Without doubt, that belief of being a failure was buried deep inside me, and it certainly did affect me so much. I'm sure that I'm not the only one to experience such feelings; maybe not a sense of failure, but there are so many other areas for us all to choose from.

So Blessed with another Father

My other father is my heavenly Father. He was there all the time, I just didn't know it. And I certainly didn't know what he was really like. Having been introduced to Jesus at a very early age and embracing him, as only a child can, he became a significant part of my life in the years that followed.

Sadly though, this heavenly Father was distant. My heavenly Father was hidden behind a solid wall of otherness: a holy God, a severe God who had to be placated by doing the right things, reading the Bible, praying every day; then, not doing so many of the things I did do.

As the years went by, my experience grew as I learned more and put it to the test. I came to understand the Trinity: Jesus the son, the Father who sent him and the Holy Spirit who empowered Jesus. Of course, I believed that the Holy Spirit was in me, like all believers should. Yes, it all fitted so well together. This was what I was teaching from the front and witnessing about all those years later.

A time came when, graciously, God set a slow burn inside me. . . For decades I'd understood and believed what Paul writes about in his letter to the Galatians in chapters three and four. Now, a profound change was taking place. I was not only believing in the fact and the positional truth, I was beginning to feel it too. I was 'knowing' it, I was experiencing it: I am his Son and it's getting to be more of a day to day reality! 'And because you are sons, God has sent the Spirit of his Son into our hearts, crying, 'Abba! Father!' So you are no longer a slave, but a son, and if a son, then an heir through God.' (Gal 4:6 & 7). My 'identity' was changing. I wanted to jump high into the air and clap my feet together! And there was so much more to discover.

Chapter 64

The Father Heart of God

Back in the the early nineteen-eighties, one of the recently published books on our shop shelves had caught my eye. An absolute plus of stocking and selling Christian books and music in Sunrise, our Truro shop, was the opportunity of the reps presenting and, hopefully, selling to us what were the up and coming publications. This particular book caught my eye and I could not wait for its publication and arrival. When it did, I grabbed a copy. It was definitely 'scratching where I was itching'.

I'd already heard of the author, Floyd McClung. He and his family were working with Youth with a Mission and living in Amsterdam's Red-Light District. I devoured the book. He starts off, 'I have written this book because most people do not know God as a loving Father.' That resonated deeply with me. I knew about it of course, but there's a gaping void between knowing what it is and living in the good of it.

Floyd covers some great stuff, all illustrated by his experiences with people in the roughest areas of Amsterdam, so many living with the real difficulties of little or no acceptance by their fathers or, even worse, children growing up never knowing a father.

Over the years I'd come to realise that I had such a good, well-meaning father but I had struggled with never feeling that I met with his approval - often with good reason, I'm sure. However the result was the same.

Floyd shared what he had discovered. One of the keys is healing for the inner damage so many of us are living with, healing that Jesus offers freely, when we are ready to face up and receive it.

It was all like a brand new revelation. I got it. This was such good news. Salvation was not just getting right with God and being born again, it could also mean that areas of my present makeup, due to my past, could be transformed. This was something to preach about. And there was even more!

Exercise can be so valuable

About ten years after this, when my week days started with a lengthy early morning run up the bank of the River Eden and back, I had my new 'toy', an Apple iPod. I had discovered that I could download talks and sermons and hear them through my earphones as I ran. I started to listen to a series of Sunday talks which Tim Keller was giving to his church in Manhattan. Straight off, I was riveted - I couldn't wait for the next mornings' run. The series was based on the Parable of the Prodigal Son, as recorded by Luke in chapter 15. It was a 'game changer' for me. Right from the outset, Keller explained that the word 'prodigal' was not in the original text but, over the years, it had come to be known as 'The Prodigal Son' because of the way the younger son hadn't waited for his father to die but demanded his inheritance, so he could enjoy it while he was young. He then squandered the inheritance on 'riotous living', hence the old-fashioned word of being 'prodigal.' To underline his point, Keller named the series 'The Prodigal Father', the real emphasis so easily missed being the ridiculously prodigal behaviour of the father.

Eventually, word had got back to the father that his son, many miles away in distant lands, was wasting his wealth rapidly, living the high life. It couldn't last forever. Every morning the father went to the top of the house, gazing into the distance to see if, just maybe, his beloved son might be returning.

Finally, the morning came and, throwing propriety to the wind, the father ran with arms wide open, dramatically demonstrated his joy at his son's return. There was no recrimination for his gross stupidity; rather, the father was demonstrating overwhelming joy at his son's final return. 'You're back! We'll all party tonight!'

The big one. The father demonstrated unconditional love - through unconditional acceptance!

What a Revelation

I'd never heard this before. I was so excited. I gave it thought, checked it out and read it in the Greek! Could it really be a parable? Yes, it was so clear, the number one point was the motivation behind why the heavenly Father had sent his son, Jesus. It was a radical demonstration of the Father's unconditional love and acceptance for all who would come to the point of facing their lostness and messed up lives; recognising that they could never qualify with a holy God by anything they could do themselves. This is unconditional love, unconditional acceptance. This is what salvation is all about!

I was so stirred as the penny dropped. Sue was the first to hear what was touching my heart, big time. It was not just that I was understanding it. I, too, am unconditionally accepted by my heavenly Father. Whether I was hitting the mark and being successful or failing miserably which, before a holy God, would

always be the way. The realisation was dawning, but this was not just a 'head' thing, I was being changed on the inside! What a wonderful heavenly Father I have. What 'Good News' of a whole different order. This is for all followers of Jesus, and especially significant for our broken world.

The God revealed through Jesus is most definitely a 'prodigal God and Father'.

Chapter 65

What is This Church Leadership About?

Fascinating. As I write this chapter today, I am provoked by my time spent this morning with Charlie and his wife, Rachel. We'd had no contact with each other for forty-eight years, when Charlie and I had both graduated from Spurgeon's Baptist College. They, very graciously, shared some of their life in churches over past decades, of God doing great things.

As church leaders they had experienced so much good, but they had also had to face and work through many times when the overseer of the group of churches in their region, had been far too heavy. The overseer was a very able man whom I also knew; he was in the same year at college as Charlie and me. The tussle for Charlie and Rachel had been coping with what seemed to be the acceptable place of leadership control, in church life, sadly, from the top down. The leadership of their overseer was black and white - do what I say or get out. A point came for the two of them when, bravely, they left behind the church they had started. Such a hard choice, but to be true to what they strongly believed, they had no regrets. They had been confronted with, what all too often, seems to be the acceptable norm of good leadership. With varying degrees of subtlety, the belief still remains that strong leadership is what works, it seems to be what people welcome as the best and it builds success!

It is certainly accepted in the business world, that good and successful leadership demands strong leadership from the top; it works and pays dividends.

Interestingly, or maybe, sadly, some of the top propagators and authors of these current leadership practices in the business world, are also Christians. It is so obvious why their principles and practices have also been acclaimed and welcomed into the area of modern church leadership: it works and it's what people want.

There is a powerful and painful snare in all expressions of leadership. The leader and the follower are both human and share the same fallen nature that is given to all of us, from the moment we were conceived. We are all vulnerable to the snare of control. For the follower, because control passes the responsibility to another who knows better than us, and we all know that it works. The result is that we abdicate and fail to find and use the gift that God has made each one of us, his children, in his church.

For the leader also, he or she is convinced that they must order and control what must happen, by whom and how, in church life, in order to bring the results that will work. Without doubt it can also fill a deep need in the leader. What a dilemma modern church life finds itself in, and what a horribly destructive thing this 'Big C' is.

It is noteworthy to remember that the roots of our modern church life were beginning to be evident in church life by the middle of the second century after the death of Jesus. Within a century that root was beginning to bear the fruit that continues to this very day, despite what the Reformation sought to bring about.

A Radical Alternative

Exploring leadership as Christians, the consummate leader has to be Jesus. We have records from four different writers in the Gospels, of the kind of leader Jesus was. There are so many varied ways in which he taught; by his actions, analogies and parables, and so often he didn't pull his punches - chatting along the way, as he and the disciples walked the many miles from village to village: Jesus was demonstrating what his Father was like in so many different ways, feeding thousands, incredible miracles, catching fish, healing many that came to him. Jesus was an amazing and captivating teacher. Jesus was an authoritative leader.

Right at the start of his ministry Jesus had to make a definitive decision during his wilderness experience for those forty days, Matthew records what Jesus went through in Chapter 4 verses 8 to 11. We read that the devil took him to a very high mountain and showed him all the kingdoms of the world and their glory, then said to him, *'All these I will give you, if you will fall down and worship me.'* Then Jesus said to him, *'Be gone, Satan! For it is written, You shall worship the Lord your God and him only shall you serve.'* Then the devil left him.

The choice that Jesus, the man, made at that point was the big departure; God the Father comes first. He willingly chose to submit to his will and walk his way. Jesus gave up the option to control. *'So Jesus said to them, 'Truly, truly, I say to you, the Son can do nothing of his own accord, but only what he sees the Father doing. For whatever the Father does, that the Son does likewise.'* (John 5:19).

Maybe, even more significant than his leadership through teaching, was the way Jesus lived, the example that he set during those three years. Jesus lived and demonstrated a different way of living, and a totally different way of leading. Finally, by the way he was tried before the Jewish leaders, then the Roman Governor Pilate and was killed, to the absolute horror of his disciples and those who loved him so much. Jesus' leadership was not exhibiting control, far from it. *'I have come to do the will of the Father.'* (Mt 26:39).

The Apostle Paul got it! From being a master controller, it took a very painful experience, being knocked off that galloping horse and then to be confronted with the sovereign God and his disapproval of how Saul had been leading his life.

Without doubt, as Saul changed to Paul, he came to understand his relationship with Jesus, the Son of God, and also the place of the Holy Spirit within the Trinity of God the Father: God the Father is the head! Through the churches that Paul initiated, across Asia Minor and Greece, with the growing pains they went through, we are privileged to have some of his letters with both Paul's correction and encouragement to the churches. How relevant they are for to us today.

The profound analogy that Paul uses about the relationship within the Godhead is to be reflected in the life and working of each local church and, also the way churches relate together across the globe: 'with all humility and gentleness, with patience, bearing with one another in love, eager to maintain the unity of the Spirit in the bond of peace. There is one body and one Spirit - just as you were called to the one hope that belongs to your call - one Lord, one faith, one baptism, one God and Father of all, who is over all and through all and in all. But grace was given to each one of us according to the measure of Christ's gift.' (Eph 4:2-6).

There is no place for a controlling concept nor practice in the church of Jesus Christ. God the Father does not do that; the love that he has for his church, in practice, is what he permitted his son Jesus to demonstrate on that cross. This is the model for the practice of his body in this earth, even now.

Frank Viola in his book 'Reimagining Church' published by David C Cook has some excellent insights into the biblical nature church and church leadership, it's well worth a read.

Chapter 66

Another Wonderful Gift

The Body

When discussing leadership it is even more important to be clear about the body, a wonderful God-given gift. The apostle Paul paints a graphic word picture when writing to the Corinthian church. He likens a local church to the human body. *'For just as the body is one and had many members, and all the members of the body, though many, are one body, so it is with Christ.'* (1 Cor. 12:12). He then goes on to apply this picture in practice to each member of the Corinthian church, leading up to verse 27, *'Now you are the body of Christ and individually members of it.'*

In the next two chapters Paul explains the relevance of this multi-gifted body. If this is true and was put into actual practice, it would be profoundly radical! Paul then goes on to apply it. Everybody has a place to function in this body. The reason and purpose for this to be put into operation is amazingly simple: for the common good, for building up, encouraging and consoling. (1 Cor 14:3). No one part of this body is more important than any other part, all are essential, for the whole body to be able to function correctly, to be healthy, to grow and *'If one part suffers, all suffer together; if one member is honoured, all rejoice together.'* (1 Cor. 12:26).

Some five or so years later, Paul writes to the Ephesian church along similar lines. *'But grace was given to each one of us according to the measure of Christ's gift.'* (Eph. 4:7).

It is not easy to live this way, so Paul writes demanding how each member of the body must relate together - in their differences. *'I urge you to walk in a manner worthy of the calling to which you have been called, with all humility and gentleness, with patience, bearing with one another in love, eager to maintain the unity of the Spirit in the bond of peace. There is one body and one Spirit.'* (Eph 4:1-4).

All this is wonderful in itself, however, it is only going somewhere when put into practice. *'Rather, speaking the truth in love, we are to grow up in every way into him who is the head, into Christ.'* (Eph 4:15 & 16). The head of this amazing, dynamic, healthy, functioning body is Jesus Christ. Jesus is the boss! If this fact is not put into practice in local churches by the leader, elder, vicar or apostle, then Jesus, the God appointed head, is being supplanted.

Jesus Modelled it

Jesus demonstrated his 'right' to be head of the Church. He lived it, as a man, in total dependence and submission to his Father in heaven. Thirty years on this earth, the Son of God demonstrated it one hundred per cent by living it out - until the heartbreaking end, on that cross. Jesus submitted to his heavenly Father, *'only doing what he saw the Father doing.'*

Jesus introduced and made clear the nature of the Trinity: Jesus was always at one with the Father - in total submission to him as the head. The Father then established Jesus the son, as head of the church, which Jesus had laid down his life for. Hence the Holy Spirit does not have divided loyalties between the Father and the Son because, as on earth and then in heaven, Jesus was and is forever one with his Father. One God not three!

When we each are functioning in our place, being built up into Christ, we are right with the head, the Father. The way the Trinity functions is the model for the way the local church is to operate also. No one role is to have pre-eminence or control over all the variety of other gifts in a local church.

Sadly, through virtually all of our church history, what Paul writes to the Corinthian church in chapters 12, 13, and 14, of his first letter, have, in practice, sadly been explained away, spiritualised, ignored or relegated to the first century only. The proper place of the gifts of the Spirit, along with all other giftings, have been completely discarded. Fascinatingly, chapter 13 has been one of the most frequently read passages of the New Testament, yet with the context of this chapter completely ignored.

Every Person Included

With the picture of a human body in chapter 14, Paul brings correction to the church, focusing on the place of spiritual gifts in the healthy church. He makes it clear that we all are gifts, and, we all have, gifts given to us by God, through his Holy Spirit. These different gifts and the expression of what we are, all have a place and a part to play, no one gift being more important than another. Just like the human body, all the different parts are absolutely essential for the body to work properly. For example, take away the liver and the result is death!

The second application is that all the parts are in submission to the head; just as it functions within the Trinity, so it is to be in the church. God the Father is the head! The way this body, the local church, works is a simple picture of how a healthy church also is to be and to function. It is to be a revolutionary demonstration of the risen Jesus and his wonderful Father to our broken world. In practice this can only work when all the gifts and parts are living in total dependence on the enabling of the Holy Spirit. No one gift is more important than another. No one gift of service that Paul refers to in Ephesians - apostles, prophets, evangelists, pastors or teachers, is more important than another. (Eph 4:11; 1 Cor:4-6). Of profound significance is the third application of this picture of the body. When it is functioning with all its varied gifts, abilities and ministries then wonderful, harmonious love is at the heart, in theory and in practice. This is the mutual love of chapter 13.

However, as we have already seen, church traditions, empowered by human logic and just plain sense, tell us someone must 'rule' and take charge; someone needs to take precedence over the rest. But if what the apostle Paul saw and expressed to the churches of his time, is truly God's view on how he wants his Body, the church, to perform, then his way is definitely not impractical or 'pie in the sky'.

Chapter 67

In Practice - When We Come Together

When we come together, what a privilege it is to sing and declare the wonder of our Creator God. What a stunning intervention his Son was, coming into our world and personal lives in such a transforming way. He is absolutely worthy of our expressed worship in all ways possible.

Building Up

There is a vital obligation we are under as Christians. Paul encourages us all, 'when we come together', by everything we say and everything we do we are to 'build each other up'. But not just when we come together as church, also in all our relationships, to use every opportunity to build one another up, *'Building up the body of Christ, until we all attain to the unity of the faith and of the knowledge of the Son of God'.* (Eph 4:13ff).

In the context of clarifying the significant place of spiritual gifts for the Corinthian church, the apostle Paul writes to them in his first letter. Repeatedly, in chapter 14, Paul uses the verb 'to build up'. There are significant attitudes expressed in the Corinthian church, but Paul does not knock the church people down, put them in their place or judge them. Rather, he seeks to 'build up' by word, action and his attitude towards them. This is the way we are all called to treat each other. The Greek word that Paul uses is 'oikodomew'. It is formed by putting two Greek words together. The first is 'oikos' which is the word for a house, a dwelling, or a household and a family. The second word is 'demo' to build. Put the two words together and it means to 'build up a house'. It gives us a great word picture. In the New Testament it is used in ten verses, always metaphorically, meaning building up and edifying. This is the task given to every member of a church; each one of us is called to play our part in all we do, to build up one another!

Encouraging

Also, in 1 Corinthians chapter 14 Paul adds two other words to our need to be building up. These words are both verbs, action words, one to encourage and the other to console.

What a challenge this is! When we are with fellow Christians, whatever the context, whether lifting the 'phone, meeting in the street, eating together or sharing a coffee during the week, we have opportunity to encourage. Maybe not quite as powerfully as relating face to face, but maybe we can use that text message, email or Facebook entry to do it. In all ways we can be building up, we can be encouraging one another. No matter what exterior we present, we all need it, all the time.

Paul makes it so clear in this chapter that meeting together is not to be just the exercise of the teaching gift, and the prophetic gift, the hospitality gift or any of the other wonderful gifts God has given to his church but, rather, it is the purpose for all of us - to build up to and also to encourage everybody. All are of equal significance and value. By the by, the Greek word used for 'encourage' is

made up of two Greek words: 'kalew' to call and 'para' the adverb, meaning
'beside'. Hence the verb 'parakalew' literally refers to being 'called alongside' someone. Interestingly, the transliteration of the Greek word 'parakalew' used in English for the Holy Spirit is 'the Parakleet', the 'called alongside one'. His role is to support, strengthen, comfort, guide and encourage the believer.

Wonderful! The Holy Spirit is the third person of the Trinity on whom Jesus chose to be totally reliant during his earthly life. The Holy Spirit was the one who took the things of the Father and made them real in Jesus' experience, through all that he had to go through. Jesus lived his life in dependence on the strengthening, comforting, and encouragement of the Holy Spirit.

What an awesome challenge. In reliance on the same Holy Spirit, we, too, are to come alongside and, similarly, encourage our fellow Christians by our actions, words and who we are. This is be the essence of what church life is to be about. But, not stopping there, just like Jesus, we are to bring genuine encouragement as well to our world today; people at work, neighbours and friends. Yes, to those who know Jesus and, just as importantly, to those who don't yet know Jesus.

As Intended To Be

God is quite capable of taking his place in his church today by directing, guiding and providing. When hearts are right and are welcoming his involvement and direction, he is quite able to speak and direct through those parts of his body as he chooses, to the benefit of his church on the earth. God is a God who speaks and a God who acts. The result, when his 'body' is working as he intends it to, is that God the Father is truly glorified on earth.

My body tells me exactly the same thing. When each organ and part of my body is working in the way it was designed to function and, also, in harmony with the rest of the body parts, I feel great! Just so, in his body, the church, we all have an equal opportunity to build up, encourage and console everyone we meet with the gift that we are. Not just on a Sunday, but every day of the week.

Chapter 68

Dynamic Living, the Normal Christian Life

Paul writes to the Christians in Colossae probably in A.D. 60, *'you have died, and your life is hidden with Christ in God'*. (Colossians 3 v 3). In the next few verses Paul tells them to put to death all the earthly aspects of their lives. He then lists a whole range of inappropriate areas in which the Colossians lived and practiced before they became Christians. Paul makes it absolutely clear that they have a choice in the matter, *'Put to death therefore what is earthly in you.'* (v 5). He follows this with the next step. They are to *'Put on then, as God's chosen ones, holy and beloved . . .'*(v 12), then follows a whole list of what is needed to be living normal Christian lives.

In Romans chapters 6 and 7 Paul paints on a larger canvas this radical change that God requires in our lives. He expands on what it is that needs to die in us. The pressure that we are all under from 'the law of sin and death', the human inevitability of being trapped and controlled by our fallen nature. The word Paul uses for this is our 'flesh', our innate humanness, since 'the fall'. We cannot help ourselves; the harder we try and feel that we are succeeding, this 'flesh' in us just pops up in a different form - pride, a sense of cracking it, finally achieving, 'we've now got this thing licked!' But this thing, 'pride', is also at the very root of our 'flesh', our broken humanity.

Paul comes to this inexorable conclusion for himself, *'so I find it to be a law that when I want to do right, evil lies close at hand. For I delight in the law of God, in my inner being, but I see in my members another law waging war against the law of my mind and making me captive to the law of sin and death. Wretched man that I am! Who will deliver me from this body of death?'* (Rom 7 vv 21-24). I can identify with Paul completely. What hope is there for me? The harder I try the worse it is! Maybe, just maybe, as Christians, we are all in the same boat: In Romans chapter eight, Paul gives us the key to dynamic living so that we may connect with our problem and make way for God's unimaginable solution.

Go on Being Filled with the Spirit

When writing to the Ephesian church the Apostle Paul offers his wonderful encouragement, *'be filled with the Spirit'.* (Ephesians 5 v 18). Paul uses the imperfect, passive tense, for the verb 'filled'. He is definitively exhorting the Christians to 'go on being filled with the Spirit.' Not just once on some special occasion, not every now and then, but all the time! It is to be a continuous active reliance upon the Spirit. He is to be the powerful, active force, in our lives. Paul is telling us that the Holy Spirit is our birthright, for all of us, male and female, as many as have received Jesus as our personal Saviour. Yes, you qualify too! This is to be our own personal experience, having exactly the same dependence that Jesus had on the Holy Spirit while he was on this earth.

Paul makes it so clear to the Corinthian church that the wonderful gifts of the Spirit are indeed also available to all, if they will receive them and exercise them to encourage and build up brothers and sisters in their walk with him, motivated by love.

It is exactly the same for all of us today; if we are really willing to receive these gifts and to exercise them for the good of others, our heavenly Father asks just one thing; in the the moment, all the time, that we, too, choose to live in dependence on Him, through the power, love and direction of the Holy Spirit, just as Jesus did when he walked the earth.

The wonderful thing about this is that it does work! But, only in the moment, when we know that we are truly dependent.

How About in Practice?

Such a good question for each one of us. Here comes that other 'Big C' again. Our heavenly Father never forces anything on us; we have to 'choose' and then be willing to trust him, and step out.

It is absolutely true, if our heart and desire is to help, support, encourage and bless somebody, then we are more than halfway there. A quick cry out to God, 'Holy Spirit give me what to say; show me what to do.' Then, maybe, the hardest part is to open our mouth and say what naturally comes, trusting that God will indeed lead us. I find it so surprising how, in the stepping out and doing it, God does give a sense of some need or vulnerability in the person or situation. If not, just what comes to mind in the moment, ninety-nine times out of a hundred, evokes a response and the conversation that follows. This is so true when talking to individuals or in church gatherings.

Chapter 69

Right Now. I Have a Future!

It's the week before Christmas. The winds from the north-west have been horrendous. Today they have subsided to 'gusty strong.' For the first time in many weeks I've ventured out to the north Cornwall coast to walk along the cliffs at Newquay. The combined effect of the sun and the vicious wind is so invigorating. I'm loving it. Walking the cliffs, looking down on the crazy surfers at this time of the year and leaning into the mighty wind in my face while I hang onto the fence post. There's such a feeling of freedom. There are very few people or any other distractions. Darn it, I've left my 'phone at home. Ok. Great!

I'm breathing in the awesome experience of the sight of those powerful waves with their multi-layers of frothy surf threatening to soak me from the beach 100 metres below. Then there's the added explosions of sound, from the force of the waves as they smash onto the jutting cliffs below. Spread out above it all, is the staggering vista of the distant multi-layered horizon, with streaks of oranges and yellows, as the sun seeks to make its impression on the dark clouds.

How could I not but respond with words of thanks and praise to my wonderful heavenly Father, who has placed me in this amazing world and given me breath to suck it all in. Soon the words run out - it's so natural and releasing to continue with the unknown language, that he has given me to praise him. Of course, I don't understand the words that are flowing on the waves of this tune, so strange to the ear. Despite all that, I have a growing sense of awe, worship and joy within me. I have no doubt that what is happening in this moment is down to him. I know it seems crazy, but I can't deny something good is happening, deep inside, as tears come to my eyes. 'I just want to continue to live to worship you, Father.'

Further along, it's time for a rest and to just gaze at those breakers, with the full force of the wind in my face. In that moment a tune and refrain comes to my mind and lips. I remembered it from when I was a teenager. It was the first song we had performed with our school house band, in front of the whole school. It was an inter-house concert competition on a Saturday evening. The song 'Blowin' in the Wind' by Bob Dylan, had been recorded by Peter, Paul and Mary, a very popular group at that time. What memories.

With a chuckle and grin on my face the words come back to me and once again I'm singing away, on the top of that Newquay cliff.

Blowin' in the Wind

How many roads must a man walk down
Before you call him a man?
How many seas must a white dove sail
Before she sleeps in the sand?
How many times must the cannonballs fly
Before they're forever banned?

The answer, my friend, is blowing in the wind
The answer is blowing in the wind

How many years must a mountain exist
Before it is washed to the sea?
How many years can some people exist
Before they're allowed to be free?

How many times can a man turn his head
And pretend that he just doesn't see?
The answer, my friend, is blowing in the wind
The answer is blowing in the wind

How many times must a man look up
Before he can see the sky?
How many ears must one man have
Before he can hear people cry?
How many deaths will it take till he knows
That too many people have died?
The answer, my friend, is blowing in the wind
The answer is blowing in the wind

Songwriter: Bob Dylan
Blowin' in the Wind lyrics © Special Rider Music

So many helpless, hopeless, disastrous situations. So much despair and brokenness in our world. So many hopes and dreams shattered. Emptiness in people's eyes, reflecting their hearts. Not just the old, the divorced, the fatherless, the homeless or the obvious casualties of our world but, progressively, all ages from pre-teens, teenagers and upwards.

The rich, the famous, the powerful, those climbing and even those who've reached the top. Many have learnt from our

culture, that to cover it all up is the only way to survive; to let it out is weakness and shame. But the heart remains a tender organ, designed and created at God's behest for the fulfilment and peace that money, success and control can not even get close to providing.

And the answer to all this? *'The answer my friend is blowing in the wind'.* As I stand leaning into that powerful force on the Newquay cliffs today, I'm thinking: 'If the words of that song are really true, then the consequences for so many in our world will be no respite, no answer or hope; the inevitable prospect is despair and its heart-breaking consequences.'

Yippee! There really is an answer: the future is a wonderful gift. It's waiting to start right now for every single person, in the present! There really is a sure and certain hope starting now. It is worth reading again what Paul writes to the Romans in chapter 8. There really is hope for our world, even today. A sure and certain future! What a gift!

Chapter 70

What is this Hope?

Another 'Big C' - Certainty!

Where does hope fit in? How do we deal with the sadness and the sense of loss we are already experiencing in life? How do we cope and face the inexorable result of death? 'This is for real Jesus. Help.'

And help he did. It had been ten years, since that correct diagnosis had been delivered, which was even worse than we had originally thought and prepared for. Getting this final conclusive diagnosis was profoundly testing. It was by far the worst for Sue, who was now facing going through total bodily disintegration. Also, so hard for teen-age girls and brothers. Watching and seeking to support, as the Sue that I had walked with through all those years, in so many varied places and experiences, was now disappearing before our very eyes. So truly heart-breaking.

As I look back and reflect, I have realised and learnt so much - the hard way. Deep searching questioning. What is this 'certain hope' I've taken so much for granted? What is this 'Good News' that I so passionately hold to? Of course before all this, life had never been easy, in so many ways. No way had I had a sheltered upbringing.I still have the vivid memories of Sue's funeral. The support was overwhelming. I was absolutely convinced: this was a demonstration of the Good News. A celebration of the star that Sue was, a celebration of her life and all the people she had cared for and influenced for good. But for me most of all it was a celebration of where she was now - at last, free from all the pain and destruction, in the presence of her maker and friend for eternity. How wonderful. The best of Good News in reality.

I was absolutely convinced of all this,. It was only later that I realised that this aspect of the Good News needs to be unwrapped - now, while we are still able to pass it on. Of course, followers of Jesus believe this, but what does hope mean? Is it just wishful thinking, is it automatic? Is it relevant when we've got another fifty years, maybe, before we need go to such areas?

Both the Old and New Testaments refer to this hope a great deal. Use your Bible Concordance and check it out! In the New Testament the apostle Paul has more to say than any other writer.

Paul is passionate about *'the glory of this mystery, which is Christ in you, the hope of glory'*. (Colossians 1:27). The proof of this hope is to be an experience for us now, made possible by the power of his holy Spirit working in us from day to day, *'for through the Spirit, by faith, we ourselves eagerly wait for the hope of righteousness.'* (Galatians 5:5).

The writer of the letter to the Hebrews writes what he desires for each of us, *'we desire each one of you to show the same earnestness to have the full assurance of hope until the end.'* (Hebrews 6:11).

Peter in his first letter includes it all in this, having been 'Born again to a living hope. *Blessed be the God and Father of our Lord Jesus Christ.'* (1 Peter 1:3).

Foundations of our Hope

The base and substance of this hope is not blind; it is based on something objective - outside of ourselves. The focus is seen in the proven death on that Roman cross, witnessed by many hundreds of people, a wide mixture; some were friends and family of Jesus and many had experienced miraculous healing through the hand of Jesus. There were also those who were vehemently opposed and hated him. His death was definitely death, for those who were expertly administering this disgusting judgement by torture were the well practiced Roman soldiers.

The resurrection of Jesus - Jesus alive in the flesh, days and weeks after his death, likewise, was witnessed by dozens of men and women who saw and touched him and even ate food with him.

Surely we have very significant grounds for putting our trust in the God who vindicated his Son, and also the words of this Jesus? By his resurrection we have the demonstration, the evidence and the proof that there is life after dying. Furthermore, we can put our trust in the reality and experiencing this for ourselves as Jesus said to Nicodemus *'unless one is born again he cannot see the kingdom of God'* (John 3:3). Check out for yourself what Paul writes about the resurrection of Jesus, in 1 Corinthians chapter 15.

To recap, this faith is more than trust in Jesus! There is another essential ingredient, that 'Big C', choice! Wonderfully, God respects our individual and personal involvement in this. There may be all the evidence in the world for faith but if we don't 'choose' to trust, it is for nought!

The combined place of faith, trusting and actively choosing, is what enables this *future hope* to come alive for us. Walking in this *hope,* can then turn to conviction! This is now my solid conviction based on my faith in who Jesus is and what Jesus did for me personally. Eureka!

When I die, I will be celebrating. I will be be in the presence of Jesus, knowing him, just as he has always known me. Join me in this celebration - what we are created for. This is fulfilment of our very being!

No New Thing

What an offer! The whole of the Old Testament in the Bible is leading and pointing to this. The fulfilment of all the old promises finally arrives when God the Father sends his Son - part of himself, Jesus. He fulfils what the Old Testament sacrifices are pointing to. Jesus, also one hundred percent man, the perfectly qualified and final sacrifice, willingly sacrifices his own life in my place and yours, and everyone who will accept it.

Three days later he's alive. In our space/time continuum! Humanly this seems so outside our possible comprehension. Jesus, the man, demonstrates that there is more to living on this planet for three score and ten years, in this 'physical world'. He opens the door for the rest of humanity to move into and to experience what it has been created for. Life on this earth, for each one of us, is intended to be just the beginning. Jesus opens the way for our ultimate fulfilment!

Certain Hope

The best and only way we can describe something outside our comprehension and completely outside our frame of reference, something like 'eternity', is only through the use of metaphor; a word picture that uses understandable images to express some aspects of the subject in mind. By definition, a picture which is one dimensional, can never get close to describing something that is multiple dimensional, the indescribable. However, this whole area of the after-life and the existence of eternity must not to be limited just to the philosophically minded and the dreamers. It's noteworthy that across the breadth of history, across all cultures, there were and still remain, a plethora of religions with a wide variety of beliefs of the nature of life on this earth and life after death.

There is indeed something rational, irrational or supra-rational within mankind that recognises, even demands, the existence of more . . . 'there must be more beyond death'. There just has to be! There is so much that points this way. The experience of my humanity with relationships, the ability to love, and the powerful and overwhelming experience of loss with its emptiness on the death of a dearly loved. The experiences of both wonderful fulfilment or destructive relational failure so often cries out from within us with despair. All this and so much more is common in our humanity. It is fascinating that even in this current age, when we have so much more knowledge and understanding of our world from science, that, when facing death, the heart cry remains the same - 'there must be more . . . there has to be!'

Profound Break In

The life, death and resurrection of Jesus breaks the inevitable mould of hopelessness like nothing else can. It has never been matched since. The first followers of Jesus had the proof of it in personal form and experience. It transformed them. Even Saul, that learned and rabid Jew, who ravaged those early Jesus followers with many deaths. On the way to fulfilling his righteous calling, Saul was knocked off his horse, blinded, shocked and totally confounded by a voice from heaven. *'Saul, why are you persecuting me?'* (Acts 9:4; 22:7; 26:14). Some thirty years later, this Saul, transformed by the living Jesus and now changed to Paul, after a long time in prison in Rome, followed in the footsteps of many before and many were to follow as Paul was put to death in that Roman prison.

This radically changed Paul died, having taught, declared and welcomed with conviction, this 'sure and certain hope' of a new life and then being face to face with Jesus. Paul was looking forward to this final fulfilment of what it had all been about for him; the reason he was put on this earth, the reason he was created, to be in personal relationship with Creator God - he was now experiencing it, way beyond the limitations of time and space. What an other wonderful 'Big C', 'Certainty'!

This Paul declared the 'sure and certain hope' so often. This hope is not wishful thinking! This hope that is guaranteed 'certain' by the resurrection of Jesus. This is also a sure fired 'certain hope' for you and me! We can have a glorious future. But, and there is a but. I, for my part, have to do something, as do all of us; it's not automatic, nor is it the reward for attending church or being a good boy or girl! On hearing, we all have to do something! Not to qualify, we can't possibly do that, nor earn qualification. Individually we must put our trust in this Jesus, who he is and what he has done, for me and you. I for one am certainly up for it!

Chapter 71

Sadness, a Wonderful Gift

God is a God of emotion! He feels and experiences emotion. It is a part of who he is - God is a God of love. *'For God so loved the world . . .'* (Jn 3:16). To illustrate the point, this love which God the Father demonstrates towards mankind in his Son Jesus, is not just an objective concept. This Father's deeply felt subjective emotion towards his one and only Son, Jesus, is also the way he feels about his wonderful creation. God loves mankind with a passion, so much so, that he was willing to send his Son, a part of himself, on a truly heartbreaking mission.

Right at the very beginning of everything, the writer of Genesis recounts how God created the earth and placed every living thing in the sea and on the earth, and then came the pinnacle of his creation,

> *'God created man in his own image,*
> *in the image of God he created him;*
> *male and female he created them.'*
> Genesis 1:27

Wonderful; man was created just like God and, in that moment, without sin. This included the gift of emotion along with it's incredible expressions - the ability to experience true love, but also anger and sadness.

The source of this love is the God who grieved so deeply over his chosen people, Israel, and the decisions they made while in the wilderness. Choosing to go their own way, they evoked great sadness and also anger, at their waywardness. Love, sadness and anger are closely related cousins! What unconscionable sadness God experienced through the way his one and only Son, Jesus, was rejected by so many people. The ultimate sadness was the Father seeing his precious Jesus hanging on that cross; following such humiliation, painful beatings and the extended agonies of a very slow death, nailed to a wooden cross.

Jesus was sent by his Father to do all that is necessary, not just for the nation of Israel, his chosen people, but to make a way that all mankind might experience the restoration and fulfilment, of all that God started in the Garden of Eden, including the experience of love with emotions and the sadness that so often results. Deep feelings of sadness in themselves are not sin. Holy God experiences the deepest of sadnesses.

So Much Grief and Sadness

Going back to that week after Sue's funeral, when I felt I needed to get away for a while, I had time to think and reflect during those many hours in the car driving to the south west.

Everything about that week had turned out to be so perfect. The weather, the scenery, the physical activity and, above all, the walking, just the two of us! Me and my heavenly Father.

All my questions, pouring out all my deep feelings of great sadness, so many lost opportunities over those past years with Sue. How our prayers and those of many others for healing seemed to

have fallen on a deaf ear. Not just sadness but tinges of anger. There was so much pent up pain inside me rising to the surface, so much I had to cope with; I was making my demands on God. If only that well meaning hospital care assistant hadn't been so foolish. It was all so unnecessary!

I found the B&B in the very small village of Lizard, on the eastern side of Cornwall's Mounts Bay. That evening, my hosts suggested for my cliff walk the next day that I leave my car at the B&B and catch the bus up the Lizard peninsular, then walk back to the Lizard Point along the cliff path. That next morning it was bright, sunny and dry. The first stage was the track down the inland lakes to Loe Bar at the coast, then to follow the cliff top path to the Lizard.

I took my time through the woods to the Bar; there was no one else around and everything was stillness, the sun was beginning to break through the leafless trees. It was so good being on my own and it just got better. I arrived at the beach, took a break to just sit on the sand and gaze out at the gentle waves, with the sun glistening across the vast expanse of Mounts Bay towards Mousehole, just visible on the horizon.

'Thank you so much, Heavenly Father. Thank you for the peace.' That experience of a sense of completion and emotional freedom is so hard to express. I just knew that all that had been happening over these tragic months, had been in his hands as, indeed, I was too, and, of course, as my Sue was, right now. An assurance swept over me as I sat on that sand, that there was more to all this than I had realised. I could have stayed there all day, but I was committed to dinner that evening at the B&B and I'd only just started, with at least another ten miles ahead of me.

From here on it just got better. The sun continued to shine all that day. The cliff path route is so full of coves, harbours and beaches, with long expanses of clifftop. There were dozens of descents from the cliffs, down steep paths to the cove below and then, of course, steep climbs up again to the cliff top.

I loved it. The opportunity to share my brokenness of heart with God was releasing. Those past years had been so incredibly hard for Sue: the mounting extreme sadness she carried, not being able to connect and support her two, precious girls as they fought their way through their turbulent teen years without their Mum; her agony with not being able to be the wonderful, caring Sue that she really was. At the same time, I also had to cope and be strong while seeing all she was going through and enduring. Sue never had a negative word to say; always that Sue smile. To this day, I wonder whether she realised just how the months had turned her wonderful smile into a twisted grimace, as she gradually lost control of her face muscles. Such great sadness. And then the awful way it had all ended.

Sadness, Peace and Completion

Not a little weary, I finally saw Lizard Point across the wide bay a couple of miles ahead, with just a wide expanse of moorland - without any more downs and ups to exhaust me further. An added delight was to walk among the friendly, but wary, Highland cattle grazing on the cliff-top open land.

Finally, I knocked on the B&B door, with sore feet and a very weary body, but with a sense of exhilaration and more than ready for that evening meal to come. This day had been such a wonderful cathartic day - the glorious sunshine and the wonderful nature all about me, but also the physical exertion and, though it seems crazy to say it, a wonderful sense of peace and intimacy with my heavenly Father. The certainty that my Sue was now in His presence transformed! I experienced a tangible sense of release. Also a wonderful peace over the way Sue had died. Release for my dear Sue. Wonderful release. She had run the race so well. What a very special lady. What a privileged man I was; the way God had shocked me, all those years before out of the blue, with that direction from God himself through that prophecy, saying that Sue was the one for me and I was the one for her.

I felt that I had to lay down all that had happened to Sue and as walked I was beginning to feel a wonderful God-given sense of peace.

What about the sadness? Yes, I walked those ten miles with sadness. Great sadness. I still have sadness. However, I've come to realise that sadness, due to really sad events and even sad choices, need not be bad. Actually there are two sorts of sadness. One sort which leads to death! (2 Cor 7:10). Humanly speaking, it is the consequence of self-centred actions and disappointed control.

There is another sadness that relates to the selfless value of another and the loving sovereignty of our God. Maybe Sue's middle name makes significant prophetic sense - 'Joy'.I am so sad for all Sue went through. I am so sad for what I lost, and for my children. For those many lost years with a suffering wife. Absolutely. Sadness, yes! But no shame for it. Far from it. Sadness is another consequence of the wonderful gift of feeling and of emotion that Creator God has given us human beings. Sadness can be a wonderful expression of worth, value and genuine love. What sort of creatures would we be if we did not have emotion? We get this from our Creator God, he experiences emotion, including sadness towards each of us who walk this earth, especially if we don't receive the priceless gift he offers in his special Son, Jesus.

However, sadness was definitely not the only thing I was so aware of, as I trekked the cliffs that day: it was 'wonder'. Glorious wonder at the value of the life Sue and I had shared together and the sure certainty ahead for both her and me: all tears wiped away.

Jesus Culture have a great song, quoting from Psalms 30 verse 5, the refrain has the words:

'Your love never fails,
There may be pain in the night -
but joy comes in the morning'

Sue spent those last ten years of her life knowing she was going to die young. As those years progressed and her bodily functions began to cease she knew death was coming.

She had made a very real decision to give her life over to Jesus in her early pre-teen years. She never went back on that decision. For her last twenty or so years Sue kept a personal day to day diary of her life. Of course, I knew she was doing that and I applauded her for sticking to it. However, I never went and read what she had written until a month ago. I could only face a little of her hard to read last years. It was so hard to read because of the content, but made worse by the way her very neat writing gradually became harder and harder to decipher, as she lost the muscle control in her hands.

To the very end, Sue knew where she was going and the final release that it was all about - Jesus, face to face and her total transformation.

Fulness of Joy. Hope fulfilled for a very special Susan Joy Reynolds - who became Susan Joy Heaton and, what better way to conclude than with the wonderful words of Matt Redman's song, 'One Day'.

One day You'll make everything new, Jesus
One day You'll bind every wound
The former things shall all pass away
No more tears
One day You'll make sense of it all, Jesus
One day every question resolved
Every anxious thought left behind
No more fear
When we all get to heaven
What a day of rejoicing that will be
When we all see Jesus
We'll sing and shout the victory

One day we will see face to face, Jesus
Is there a greater vision of grace
On that day
And one day we'll be free, free indeed, Jesus
One day all this struggle will cease
And we will see Your glory revealed

On that day
And when we all get to heaven,
What a day of rejoicing that will be
When we all see Jesus,
We'll sing and shout the victory
Yes, when we all get to heaven
What a day of rejoicing that will be
And when we all see Jesus
We'll sing and shout the victory
Oh one day, one day
Yes, one day we will see face to face, Jesus
Is there a greater vision of grace?
And in a moment, we shall be changed
Yes, in a moment, we shall be changed
In a moment, we shall be changed
On that day

When we all get to heaven
We'll sing and shout the victory. We will weep no more
No more tears, no more shame, No more struggle, no more
Walking through the valley of the shadow. No cancer, no depression
Just the brightness of Your glory. Just the wonder of Your grace
Everything as it was meant to be. All of this will change
When we see You face to face. Jesus, face to face.

Songwriters: Matt Redman / Beth Redman / Leonard
Jarman
One Day (When We All Get To Heaven) lyrics © Capitol
Christian Music Group
Album: Glory Song

Prologue

I have lived through a period of radical change. Societal change, cultural and attitudinal change to God. I've witnessed the profound changes resulting from the First World War through the effects on my grandparents, followed by the Second World War, which led to the radical developments that have affected the globe exponentially.

Half-way through the last century, most British people would have viewed themselves as 'Church of England', even if attendance was limited to funerals and marriages. Even that has changed dramatically as we've entered the 21st century. For so many people now the concept of a Creator God is absurd and irrelevant to life today.

Wonderfully, this Creator God, with his Son, Jesus, and the Holy Spirit, have not been wrong-footed! During my life-time, he has been taking the opportunity to break his Church out of the historical straight-jacket it chose to don in the early centuries of church history.

Across the globe are expressions of a dramatically changing understanding of what church is, and the meaning and practice of relationship with the Father, the Son and the Holy Spirit, as well as relationship between fellow Christians.

This amazing, loving God, has only just started in turning this on-going period of change to good. As despair and hopelessness continues, many people groups will see living examples of hope and new life through a whole new expression of Christianity in practice and the dynamic living church of Jesus Christ.

'As darkness becomes more intense the light shines even brighter.'

Bring it on God.

And just a final reminder - those Big 'C's:

Control - Choice - Certainty

Coming to the End

What an amazing journey my life has been. So many dramatic changes, different nations, so many tough times with deep pain and regrets, yet learning so much the hard way. There have also been so many wonderful experiences with outstanding blessings from a wonderful heavenly Father.

O yes, I mustn't forget the biggest and best 'Big C' of all: Jesus the 'Christ'!

I am now totally convinced . . . . . the best is yet to come, for eternity!

THE END

Printed in Great Britain
by Amazon